Reflections of an American Muslim

Shahid Athar

Foreword by
Mahmoud Abu-Saud

Library of Congress Cataloging in Publication Data

Athar, Shahid
    Reflections of an American Muslim

    Includes bibliographical references.
    1. Islam I. Athar, Shahid II. Title

ISBN: 0-934905-26-6

BP
16.2
1.2
.A78
1994

Distributed by
KAZI Publications, Inc
3023 W. Belmont Avenue
Chicago IL 60618
Tel: 312-267-7001; FAX: 312-267-7002

Contents

In the Name of God, Most Kind, Most Merciful

"You are the best of peoples,
evolved for mankind
enjoining what is right,
forbidding what is wrong
and believing in God." (3:110)

*****

To my father, who taught me
honesty, hard work and simplicity
To my mother, who never missed her prayers
in spite of her illness
To my wife, for her encouragement and understanding
To my children, for their love of Islam
To my teachers for their patience with my ignorance
May God be pleased with all of them.

PREFACE

One may wonder why a busy physician should write about Islam. For me, while living in a non-Muslim society for over two decades, Islam became a necessity, a way of life to live by and show to my children. I had to learn Islam myself to teach my children as there were not Islamic teachers around. I was frequently called by schools, organizations, both Muslim and interfaith groups, radio and TV stations, to present and defend Islam. Being a physician, I was qualified not only to diagnosis the diseases of the body, but of the soul, as well. I could easily recognize the ailments of the American society and the Muslim community with which I lived. Thus, at the request of my friends, I decided to compile my speeches in a book form, many of which have been published elsewhere. For practical purposes, I have used Yusuf Ali's translation of the Quran. The book has been arranged into five sections dealing with social, educational, political, missionary and practice concerns for Muslims. However, it is not intended for Muslims alone. Many non-Muslims will find these articles interesting and informative. It has been written in an easy to read American English.

I pray for the soul of my mentor, Dr. Mahmoud Abu Saud, who reviewed and wrote the foreword. I thank my secretaries, Juliet, Barbara, Beth and Martha for typing these articles during busy patient days and I thank my publishers, KAZI Publications of Chicago for publishing this book.

Shahid Athar, M.D.
Indianapolis, IN
November 1, 1994

FOREWORD

It is rare to meet with a book whose contents reveal the character of its author in such clarity as in this book. Every page reflects a part of the author's deep belief and genuine conviction. If ever I try to compose an expressive picture of Shahid Athar, I would not have been able to draw a better one than that delineated by the words of this book.

The reader will immediately discover that the author, in his humble endeavor, did not intend to write about Islamic jurisprudence or any other Islamic discipline. He is concentrating on the basic factor that exalts the human being, that distinguishes him from a lower species, and that makes him fit to live in a better community. He is after the human being's belief and faith. The only way to achieve this is submission to the Creator.

The approach to the different problems that a person may encounter in the course of attaining such faith are subjective. The author tells us that one cannot acquire "piety" and true faith by means of listening to preachers or even reading books, alone, but that they need to be enhanced through personal experience and individual efforts.

In any given society, if the individual is acting in conformity with a sublime ethical code—a code that is revealed through a Messenger and a Prophet, then one can be ascertained of having a peaceful society of well being. In simple eloquent language, the author indicated the draw-backs of the secular society in which he lives. In earnest logic he cautioned Muslims against the modern American amorality and permissiveness. His courage and sincerity emanating from his deep convictions and wide experience bestow on his writing the beauty and the fortitude that are unique and genuine.

Mahmoud Abu-Saud
Panama City, Florida

PART I:
SOCIAL CONCERNS

"O you who believe!
Save yourself and your families from a fire,
whose fuel is men and stones,
over which are (appointed) angels, stern and severe,
who fail not (from executing)
the commands they receive from God,
but do (precisely)
what they are commanded" (66.6).

1 THE AGONIES OF A MUSLIM IN A NON-MUSLIM SOCIETY

INTRODUCTION

I have been living in the United States for the last twenty-five years. When I left my homeland as a young man, the important thing on my mind was to leave a land of "lesser opportunity" to go to a land of "greater opportunity" and "to be something." Now that I have achieved that in the sense that I am a well-established physician, known and respected in my community, have a wife and four children, I have a moment to pause and ask, "Where I am? Who I am? Where I am going?" As it has been said, "If you don't know where you are going, you are sure to end up in a place where you never wanted to be." I am going to share with the readers some of my observations and experiences of my stay in the United States to show that the situation has improved in the last quarter of a century.

THE PRACTICE OF RELIGION

The truth is very few missionary delegations from overseas, whose sole purpose is the preaching of Islam, become residents of this country. Rather, they come for a week or so and then leave. They do not live here. On the other hand, for many Muslims who do choose to live here, the practice of Islam is merely a habit that they have acquired from their fam-

3

ily back home rather than a way of life for the sole purpose of pleasure of God Almighty.; Although, there is no restriction on the practice of religion in this country, the environment is not always as favorable to new faiths as it may seem. For example, offering the noon prescribed prayers at work is difficult for most Muslim employees. Several cases have been recorded in which a Muslim was fired from his job for practicing Islam during lunch hour. It was called "doing Yoga." Another pious Muslim used to lock himself in a rest room and perform his prescribed prayer for fear of being seen. Not every American city has a community center or a mosque. Even those with such facilities are not active five times a day, seven days a week. Most of the activities are confined to Friday prescribed congregational prayer and Sunday school. What about Ramadan, the month of the prescribed fast? Even it one is performing the prescribed fast, one may not sense that this is the month of Ramadan in the same way that one would will sense in a Muslim country. Some Muslims who do perform the prescribed fast, do so alone. They eat the post-sunset meal of the prescribed fast alone and perform the Special Night prayer (*tarawih*) of Ramadan alone. The day of the Festival marking the end of the month of prescribed fasting feels a little better, but there are only 24 hours in a day. For an immigrant Muslim, the joy of the end of Ramadan is overshadowed by the sadness of being away from ones home and family. Therefore, a Muslim living in a non-Muslim society can practice his or her religion, and may do it with hardship, but the joy of being a Muslim is often not there. The prevailing feeling is more one of a lonely rose of faith, surviving, in a spiritual desert.

AGONIES ABOUT FOOD CONSUMPTION

For those Muslims who do want to preserve their faith and follow its dietary laws, life is sometimes difficult. Again it is not due to the non-availability of permissible (*halal*) food. In big cities permissible meat is available and in smaller towns, if a Muslim wants, the believer can and sometimes does drive to a bigger city to obtain permissible meat. The problem is acute when one has to eat out. Nearly everything is contaminated with lard. This includes vegetable soup, salad, fried chicken, hamburger, cheese, etc. Even if they say they use vegetable shortening, still they might have used the same frying pan and utensils for frying both kinds of food. Similarly, alcohol is used in many punches, sauces, and other delicacies and liquid based medicines. It took me one year to discover Pepperidge Farm bread which uses vegetable shortening.

CHILDREN'S EDUCATION AND THE INFLUENCE OF THEIR PEERS ON THEIR MORALS

In this highly technological society, is not difficult to gain a professional education while, at the same time, it is difficult to obtain an Islamic education. Muslim children spend forty hours a week under care of non-Muslim teachers, surrounded by non-Muslim friends and yet parents expect them to practice Islam. One hour a week of Sunday school's Islamic education or making them recite a few words or verses is not enough to withstand the influence of their peers. Children are greatly influenced by their friend's behavior. In this society, where use of drugs, alcohol, pot, rock music, and illegitimate mixing of sex is so common in high school children, how can we save our children from such influences? Should we stop them from going to school? Should we stop them from mixing with their American neighbor, or should we send them back to their Muslim country of origin—a serious question for Muslim parents. One answer is to practice our faith ourselves in the best way we know how, constantly learning about things we had not known about Islam. We can then become models for our children if we teach them how to reason and not force religion upon them. By teaching them how to reason, they can reason with themselves that they do not want the results of what they see going on around them. They want a better life for themselves.

SOCIAL LIFE FOR MUSLIM MEN

It is said: "The human being is a social animal," and "No human being is an island." Therefore, social encounter is essential for the psychological well being of a person. What opportunities does the non-Muslim society provide? When American men get together, they usually talk about baseball, football, women and interest rates, while drinking beer and wine. These things may not generate interest in a Muslim man who has not grown up in this society. He may feel isolated and alone among them. Thus, it is necessary to form communities or join in with other communities of people who share other interests.

SOCIAL LIFE FOR MUSLIM WOMEN

She is much different from her non-Muslim counterpart whether or not she is a professional or someone who works. An American woman married or single has many friends of both sexes, at work and in her neighborhood, to whom she can talk about the latest fashions, super market sales, men in their life and other items of mutual interest. They go together for swimming, racket ball, tennis and exercise spas. This is again not necessarily a life pattern that an immigrant Muslim woman might choose. The immigrant Muslim women often do not speak English well, so they are unable to communicate with the neighbor's wife over what's cooking in each other's house, children, marriage, etc. They also become isolated from the society in which they live.

THE HOSTILITY OF THE MEDIA TOWARD THE MUSLIM WORLD AND ISLAM

This is a painful issue for a sensitive Muslim. It is not so much so for someone who is only interested in the sports column of newspapers or in on-going sales. However, those Muslims looking for news items in American newspapers are disappointed since the media is often anti-Islam, anti-Muslim and frequently publishes fabricated and distorted news about Islam and the Muslim world such as given head lines, "Young Lovers Hanged in Pakistan," "Princess Shot Dead in Saudi Arabia for Adultery," "Pakistan Making Atomic Bomb for PLO," "Kaddafi Sends Hit Team to the U.S.A. (they still have not arrived)!" Those who read the columns of Joseph Kraft, Jack Anderson and Paul Harvey know what I am talking about. Even in social gatherings, it is difficult for a sensitive Muslim to listen to all this. I will give you an example of a high society social event which I had to attend to in my official capacity in 1982. The discussion is true and went like this:

Mrs. X: Dr. A, what do you think of Khomeini? Don't you agree that this old man is crazy and a murderer?

Dr. A: Well, Mrs. X., he might have committed some excesses, but I do not think that he murdered people like the ex-shah did.

Mrs. X: But the Shah was our friend., Don't you realize how much he did for his country? Those idiots (Iranians) should not have resisted his development and modernization efforts Those people deserve what they got (bullets).

Dr. A: (Remains silent after realizing that a tyrant murderer, if he is a "friend" of the U.S.A. is supposed to be acceptable "to us" (Americans). The topic changes.)

Mrs. X: And what about that mad man Kaddafi? Don't you expect that this man will be a disaster for the entire world if that insane fanatic gets a hand on an atomic bomb?

Dr. A: Look Madam X, I do not like Kaddafi and I am not defending him, but the historical point is that the first atom bomb actually used to destroy millions of human beings were used not be a fanatic mad man but a sane American President named Truman!

Mrs. X: But we used atom bomb in Japan to stop war, to restore peace in the world, to prevent more killing afterwards.

Dr. A: I agree, but why did you not use the same atom bomb on the German front for the same reasons? Just because that would have killed people of your own color and race instead of the yellow race of Asia.

This made Mrs. X very upset and she quietly moved onto another table. Dr. A could not talk on the subject of beauty, sex, wine, interest rates, and baseball, so he left the party.

In conclusion, the agony of Muslims living in a hostile non-Muslim world is great. They are living in a spiritual desert, in a social vacuum, trying to think all by themselves. Someone may ask, "So why do they stay?" The fact is that as Muslims, they believe in the same values for which this country was founded. In other words, they feel closer to the founding fathers than what America has become. Time will tell how important it was that those Muslims who have the strength of character to withstand the agonies remain in America to re-instill the American values of which the Americans themselves have lost.

2 OBSTACLES TO THE COHESION OF MUSLIM UNITY

God says in the Holy Quran, *"When comes the help of God and victory and you see the people enter God's religion in crowds, celebrate the praise of your Lord, and pray for his forgiveness, for He is oft returning in grace and mercy"* (Nasr:110).

It is true that Islam is the fastest growing religion in the USA. There are presently about six million Muslims here. As a result, the number of Muslim organizations is growing at the same rapid rate. Every large American city presently has several Muslim organizations and mosques.

Building a mosque is a prophetic tradition. The first thing Prophet Muhammad (ص) built when he migrated from Makkah to Madinah in 622 CE was to build a mosque. However developing a community around the same area and attached to that mosque is more difficult. In 1915 before the Communists occupied Muslim Russia, there were 24,000 mosques. When their form of government collapsed in 1992, there were only 423 mosques, most of which were locked during week days.

In my opinion, it is easier to built a mosque than it is to build a community to support it. All you need to build a mosque is a donor, or a group of donors, the purchase of a piece of land and bricks, and the hiring of an architect to put them together. However, the unit of a community, human beings, differ from the bricks. You cannot buy them. You have to win their heart with respect and service. You join them with love and not cement.

While Muslims in America have been successful in building mosques

9

and organizations—for example in New York state alone there are 150 mosques—we have failed in bringing Muslims together. The first problem I see with American Muslims today is the development of a self-interested ego. We are living in a "me first" society whose motto is "I will get me a hamburger." Therefore, Muslims have developed this ideology, "Not only will I not cooperate with you, but I will ignore you because I don't like you, but when I want to do the same thing that you are trying to do, I want you to support me."

A faith should be able to bring people together, rather than to chase them out and this is what Islam promotes, but once American Muslims adopt the western ego of self-interest, they lose Islamic values. An extension of this problem is an attitude which is selective of the Traditions (*ahadith*) of Prophet Muhammad (ﷺ). The Traditions are referred to when they want to stop someone from doing something, but they do not apply the same criterion to themselves. They say, for instance, "Whatever you are doing is un-Islamic because there is such and such a Tradition (*hadith*) which says so and so." When they want to do the same thing, they say, "I see nothing wrong with doing such and such because there is nothing in the Quran or Traditions which oppose it."

The second problem can be stated by in terms of three types of situations: There are those who are making things happen, those who watch things happen and those who don't know what happened. We Muslims not only belong to this third class of the pathetic group, but we have added a fourth group, as well: Those who criticize every thing that happens. When rice is being cooked, we want to stay away from the heat, but when it is being served, we want to complain of the shortage of salt, sugar, raisins and almonds. This can be illustrated by a story told to me by my close friend in Panama City, Florida. After he led the prescribed prayer, someone came from behind and told him that the prescribed prayer was invalid, because "your nose did not touch the ground during prostration." He said to the gentleman, "I am an old man who has had a heart operation. Perhaps my nose was not touching the ground during prostration, but may I know what was your nose doing then?" We should not accept criticism unless it is accompanied by a desire and commitment to improve the situation by the critics themselves.

Participation: When an organization invites a community to participate, does it mean it? Or does it say, "Say nothing. Do nothing. Just send your check in the mail." We should not accept donations without active participation. When we Muslims do missionary work and by the mercy of God, non-Muslims accept Islam, we should not leave him/ her alone. We should make him/her a part of the family, a brother or sister by Quranic ties, and help the new Muslim to become a self supporting citizen.

All these problems have a common root. I asked a 14 year old what the number one problem affecting Muslims today is? I was expecting her to say, "Lack of unity," but she loves to disagree with her dad, and she is usually right. She said, "We Muslims don't love each other." She is right. Even if we do, for some reason, we cannot express it. We don't speak well of each other. To the contrary, our Prophet used to greet each Companion so warmly and showed such affection that each of them thought he loved him the most. He has said in an authentic Tradition, "None of you will enter Paradise until you have faith, and you will not complete your faith until you love each other" (Muslim). And, "On the Day of Judgment when there will be no shade other than the shade of God. One of the six categories of Muslims who will receive shade under the Throne will be those who love one another just for the pleasure of God" (Muslim).

Remember what God Almighty has said in Quran: *"And He has put love between their hearts. Even if you had spent all that is in the earth, you could not have produced that love, but God has done it, for He is Powerful, Wise"* (8.63). *"And hold fast by the rope of God all together and be no disunited. Remember the favor of God on you when you were enemies, then He joined your hearts so by His favor you became brothers. You were on the brink of a pit of fire, then He saved you from it; thus God makes clear to you His Signs so that you may follow the right way"* (3:103).

It is not unnatural for Muslims to develop an organization based on geographical locations within a city, or even on the basis of language or ethnic origin, as if God created humanity of the same color, appearance, and speaking the same language! He says in the Quran, *"Oh you mankind, we created you from a single (pair) of a male and a female, and made you into nations and tribes, that you may know each other (not that you may despise each other). Verily in the sight of God, the most honored of you is the most righteous of you, and God is full of knowledge, and is well acquainted"* (49:13).

In one authentic Tradition, Prophet Muhammad (ص) has said, "A Muslim is a mirror to another Muslim" (Abu Daud). What he meant was that we have an obligation to point to fellow Muslim his shortcoming and to tell the truth about his good aspects. He did not say, "A Muslim is a sword (in correcting the mistakes) of another Muslim. A mirror has the following qualities, that we also should have when reflecting upon other fellow Muslims. A mirror has a one-to-one relationship with an object. It does not announce a defect in public; a mirror does not backbite, but we do; a mirror does not distort the image, but gives an honest, unbiased picture. Neither does it exaggerates nor does it belittle the object; and, an object goes to the mirror. The mirror does not travel looking for the shortcomings of the object.

Therefore, in order to bring Muslims together I suggest the following: Accept each other as we are. Be gentle in criticism and generous in appreciation.Love each other and speak good of each other as much as possible to each other's face and behind their backs. Before we expect an organization to do anything for us we should ask what we have or what we can do for the organization; while criticizing, we should ask ourselves: Am I doing this to prove that I am right? Or for the sake of the community? Is my action going to bring the pleasure of God or of Satan? Am I a part of the solution? Or part of the problem in my mosque or organization?

Finally, we must ask ourselves, how far we are willing to go to bring Muslims together, sacrificing the glory of self, race, ethnic background, language, nationality, etc. for the glory of God Almighty.

I end this with the short *surah* which is the essence of Quran, and which the worthy companions used to say to each other when departing.

"By the token of time
the mankind is in the loss
except for those who have
true belief and pure actions,
and join together in the mutual teaching of
truth and perseverance."

3 Social Concerns of Muslims in North America

God has said in the Quran, "*All of you who believe, save yourself and your family from a fire whose fuel is man and stone, over which are appointed angels, stern and strong, who resist not God's command but do what they are ordered to do*" (66:6).

I begin this discussion with a story. There was a boat with two decks or levels and there were passengers on both levels. The boat was traveling quietly down the river. Suddenly, someone from the lower deck went to the top deck and said, "Do you know what is happening on the lower deck?" The people on the upper deck asked what was happening on the lower deck. He said, "The lower deck ran out of water. There is no drinking water and you know what they have found to be the solution to take care of their water shortage? They have drilled a hole in the bottom of the boat to get water." The people on the upper deck said, "So what. It is their problem on the lower deck and they have found their own solution for this. We have plenty of water so we don't have to worry about it."

When the water entered the lower deck, it also sank the people on the upper deck because the whole boat sank in the river. Thus, the social problems of this country are also the social problems of Muslims, even if Muslims are not involved and even if it is not affecting them at this time. The following are problems that American Muslims have to address now or later:

1. Strengthening their family life. We need an intact family in order

to survive. Therefore, a strong family institution is the basis of the Islamic community.

2. We have to take care of ourselves physically. We Muslims are not that good in taking care of our health ourselves and therefore they are not prepared to meet a crisis if one comes.

3. We have to have excellence in education.

4. We have to be financially independent.

5. We have to provide equal opportunities for women. It is not enough to talk about women's rights. They have to be given their due share in all of the levels possible including community organizations and jobs.

6. We have to develop a support system for the elderly because we are going to become elderly and we don't know whether we will end up in nursing homes or there will be some retirement homes built around a mosque where we will be able to live peacefully. We have to also take care of the widows and orphans because it has been commanded to us by God. We have to take care of those who are poor, homeless and needy.

7. We have to develop an Islamic perspective on issues affecting our American society including abortion, teenage pregnancy, alcohol and drug abuse, homosexuality, AIDS, right to life, poverty, and child and wife abuse.

One of our problems is how to develop self-esteem for Muslims. We have been labeled as terrorists, hijackers, and backward people. Anytime anything happens in the society, which is bad, like a murder or a bombing of a building, either Muslims are blamed or framed for that and we are made to feel bad. We know that there are a lot of crimes that happen otherwise in the society. There are close to 100,000 rapes a year, close to 23,000 murders every year, millions of thefts a year, but no one says that those people who are committing all of these crimes are Christians or Jews which, in fact, they are. Now, Islam is being judged according to the actions of a few bad people and we are all made to defend Islam for the wrongdoing of a few. So how do we feel good about ourselves? How do we promote the good image of Islam? This is something to question. We can do this by being a good Muslim, by showing Islam through our example, by telling non-Muslims that Islam is a way of life and a Muslim is in a state of being in Islam or a state of submission to the Will of God. So self-esteem depends upon the degree to which we are a Muslim. Therefore, those who are trying to defame Islam by their non-Islamic actions should have no effect on us. Non-Muslims should not judge us by their actions.

We also have to have good relationships with non-Muslims on a personal level. We should show them that we do care for all Americans and their social needs and their problems because we are also Americans. When we are advised through the Traditions to take care of our neighbor, they do not say that those neighbors have to be Muslim. Therefore, we should present Islam in a way that it creates a good image of us and our religion.

One of the major concerns should be the education of ourselves, our family and our children. We live in a society where education interestingly enough is not very much emphasized. Up to 25% of U.S. high school students drop out every year nationally and they are doing very poorly on the international level in many fields. For example, in the area of geography, of 9 developing countries including Sweden, Germany, Japan, Canada, Italy, France, U.K., and Mexico, the U.S. was at the bottom out of a possible 16 correct answers in a question of geography. American students gave only 6.9 correct answers, the lowest of all the other countries. In science, out of close to 20 countries, American students were number 17 and their score was 16.5 while the highest score was 21.7. I am saying all of this because if we leave Muslim children in the public school system and do not make enough effort to improve their education, they will become like the rest of the Americans with very minimal knowledge acquired to compete with the rest of the world. In fact, it has been shown that children of immigrants are not doing as good in terms of education or job placement as their parents who came from less-developed but more hard-working countries.

What about poverty in this country? This country, so rich, so big, so powerful, has the highest number of big houses and also the highest number of homeless people. One out of every 5 children in the U.S. lives in a household with an income level below the poverty level. Compared to international standards, the U.S. leads Sweden, Germany, the Netherlands, France, the U.K., Australia and Canada in the number of children at poverty level and the number of elderly who are impoverished. Just to give an example, in Sweden, 1.6 percent of the children live in poverty and 4.3 of the elderly live in poverty, but in the United States, the figures are 20.4 and 10.9 respectively.

The problem of poverty is affecting ethnic minorities more than the white Anglo-Saxon class. After the generation of Muslim doctors and engineers, who are well-placed now, has passed, if Muslim children are not able to establish themselves, then they may also slip into the level of poverty.

The next social concern in the present society is the lack of intact families. 25% of children have only one parent living with them who has to also earn a living so the children are being raised by television, the so-called "latch kid syndrome." Again, the U.S. leads all of the developing countries in the number of children who are being raised by single parents. The percentage for the U.S. is 26-% as compared to Japan at 5 %. Thus, it is so important for Muslim families to have intact families in which one of the parents is able to take care of the children while the children are young when the other parent works.

The next issue I want to address is alcohol and drug abuse in this country. According to the 1988 figures, close to 18 million Americans use marijuana, 15 million are alcoholics, 5.5 million use cocaine, 2 million are heroin addicts and 6 million are addicted to prescription drugs. The number of drug offenders per 100,000 of the population in the United States, is more than 20 other developing countries. The figure for the U.S. is 346 while the figure for example of, the United Kingdom is 56 and Japan is 1. The United States has a big appetite for cocaine and marijuana and again, it leads 30 different Western countries in this craving. The amount of marijuana consumed in the United States is 3,485 kilos per million population and 38.1 kilo of cocaine. For Japan, this figure is 1.6 for marijuana and none for cocaine. 25% of high school children in this country consume marijuana, 6.7 percent are on LSD, 2.5 percent are on cocaine and 0.3 percent are on heroin. The drug problem is costing this country large amounts of money which should have been spent on social welfare. $110 billion is involved in drug trafficking; $117 billion is lost in lost revenue and treatment of alcoholism; and $2.5 billion was allotted by Congress to fight the drug problem.

There are 10,000 cocaine children born every year. Each cocaine child, that is, a child that is born to a cocaine addicted mother, costs about $100,000 per month in a newborn nursery care. Interestingly enough, $20 million is spent every year in advertisements for alcohol and the U.S. is also the No. 2 producer of marijuana.

I am saying all of this because if we are going to leave our children to mix with those children who are on drugs or play basketball with children who are on drugs, then it is possible that our children will also get this habit because of peer pressure.

Violence is also a major problem in our society. Close to 20 %of the people are victims of violence once in their lifetime. This country again leads the rest of the civilized world in the number of murders committed per year. Washington, D.C. is not only the political capital, but is also the drug and murder capital of the world. In the United States, 23,438 people were killed in homicides in 1990 compared to 139 in Austria and 34 in Finland. Again, for some of the other most advanced countries like Australia and England, the figure is close to 2,000.

There have been surveys conducted in high schools with metal detectors that students have to pass and many students have been found to carry different weapons—knives, guns, chains, and other items. The number of violent crimes and homicides is much higher among black youth. The greatest danger to black youth in America is not from a white policeman, but from another black youth.

One of the reasons behind the violence in our society is television. Television, by showing violence, promotes violence. An average child watching 2 hours of television a day is exposed to 9,000 acts of violence per year. This violence is shown not only on the television, but also in recorded music. Many of the heavy metal types of rock music preach nothing but sex and violence and, in fact, there is the suggestion that in some of the rock music, there is subliminal, or unconscious, suggestion to induce violence such as a Satanic cult. This has again trickled down even to comic books. Thus, if we see violent behavior in Muslim children, it is not their own fault as the nature originated by God in all children is corrupted through the nurturing process. Children become what they see, what they hear and what kind of people they are with.

Another problem in the society, especially in the youth, is of sexual promiscuity. 54% of high school children are sexually active and the number increases as they increase in their grade. By the twelfth grade, 72-% said in a popular survey that they had had sex. So if you visit the hallways of high schools, you will see acts of kissing and other socialization openly taking place. Again, an average child watching TV for 2 hours a day is exposed to TV programs per year with 5,000 sexual suggestions as we see in soap operas and other programs and therefore, it gets into their brain that sexual activity is a normal part of development.

What does this increased sexual activity lead to or result in?

1. There is a high number of teenage pregnancy in this country. Close to 1.5 million teenagers become pregnant annually. The numbers are higher both among whites and black and both in upper and lower socio-economic groups. Interestingly enough, the United States, which spends more money on sex education than other developing countries, still has the highest pregnancy rate, higher than France, Canada, Sweden, and the Netherlands.

Let's talk about dating. Dating has become a part of normal social development in this country. A girl who does not date is considered some-times anti-social. In fact, teachers have sometimes told parents of Muslim girls in high school that their daughter is abnormal because she does not socialize and although many boys want to date her, she has refused. When a young boy and a young girl go out on a date, it is not as it used to be in the old days. Maybe not on the first date, but soon thereafter, the date results in having sex. But apart from the sex, there are many other things that can happen to girls when they go out on dates. One of them is date rape just as was alleged in the Smith-Kennedy case in Florida. Nearly all of the unreported and one-third of the reported rapes in this country, which were 100,000 in 1990-91 according to Newsweek, were committed by a current or former boyfriend.

This country, which has given women so many rights now, and women's liberation, which has come to a peak, has not been able to pro-tect them from the evils of society. It has a large number of women, over 100,000, who are raped every year. Only 10 % of rapes are reported, so the actual number is much higher. And, again, compared to 20 different Western countries, the United States leads in the number of rapes report-ed per 100,000 women. The number for the U.S. is 114, in the U.K. it is 9 and in Japan it is 7, in Ireland it is 4.

This high number of teenage pregnancies and other pregnancies leads to abortion. The name, abortion, should be changed to infanticide. In this country, close to 1.2 million living fetuses are aborted every year. Since 1973, 30 million living fetuses have been murdered. Of 4.5 million live births in this country, 1.6 million or close to one-third, are the result of out-of-wedlock or illegitimate pregnancies. Abortion makes no distinc-tion in terms of class. Of all economic levels, it is affecting in terms of 25 to 30 %. It is 18.5 % in the married population and 63.3 % in unmarried. population and 33 % non-whites and 67 % in whites, 31.5 % are Catholics and 41.9 % are Protestants. In this survey, 22 % of Americans said that they did not belong to a particular religion or they were atheists. Again the United States is leading the world, not only in the number of teenage pregnancies, but also in the number of abortions. The number is higher than in Britain, Canada, France, Sweden, and the Netherlands.

Another danger of premarital or extra-marital sex is sexually transmitted disease. The annual incidence of syphilis in this country is 130,000, gonorrhea 1.4 million, chlamydia 4 million, pelvic inflammatory disease 420,000, genital herpes 500,000, Hepatitis B 300,000 and AIDS over 200,000.

Now that I am on the subject of AIDS, I want to speak in more detail about this. It is not true that it is a disease of only homosexuals. Thus far, Muslims cannot just say that since they don't practice homosexuality, they are immune from this disease One can get AIDS from blood transfusions, IV drugs, or heterosexual contact with an AIDS patient or handling the excrement of an AIDS person.

Therefore, there many ways of getting AIDS. It is a world-wide epidemic now. The incidence of HIV virus world-wide is: United States, 1 million; South America, 1 million; Africa, 6 million; Southeast Asia, 500,000; Australia, 30,000; Soviet Union, 20,000; China, 20,000; and Europe, 500,000

The total number of HIV infected people in the Middle East is only 30,000. HIV infection is the carrier state and will manifest itself in due course, maybe in 10 years, and may manifest as the AIDS syndrome in 10 years. Again, the U.S. is leading all the civilized world in the number of actual AIDS cases. The number of AIDS cases has increased to 202,000 as of 1991 and it is increasing at a geometric proportion. The number of AIDS, for example in Japan, another developed country, is only 405. Out of the 10 million infected world-wide with HIV, 900,000 are children and newborns who got AIDS, not through the practice of homosexuality, but through their mothers who were either drug abusers or partners of AIDS cases. More than 55 % of all of the AIDS cases in the United States reported so far, have already died. It is projected that by 1996, the number of AIDS in this country will double. Of all the 21 Muslim countries in the Middle East, the total population is close to half a billion. Only 366 AIDS cases have been reported so the lifestyle of non-practicing homosexuality does help. Of all these 355 cases, again many are imported cases just like they import Western cars and Western weapons and cosmetics, so they visit the casinos of Las Vegas, Reno, and other resorts in Europe and they bring back home a gift for their wives.

AIDS is a really terrible disease to have. It destroys the immune system totally so that the body has no defense against any infection. I have seen a few AIDS patients who have been in terrible physical shape, either from the disease or from the treatment. The life expectancy, after acquiring the disease, is only five years. The cost of one treatment of AZT alone is $8,000 per year.

The cost of education and prevention of AIDS in this nation is $10,000 per person and although many people are dying of cancer and heart disease, only 3.5 dollars per person is being spent on cardiac rehab and education and $185.00 per person is being spent on cancer prevention. On the other hand, for example, in 1990, 800,000 Americans died of myocardial infarction, The point I am making is that much of our money which should go for social reform and preventive health is going to AIDS which could have been prevented if we had changed our life style at an earlier time. Prophet Muhammad (ﺹ) has said, "When sin afflicts people and they publicize it, then God subjects them to ailments unknown to their forefathers" (reported in Tirmidhi).

AIDS was not known to us 10 to 15 years ago. It was when homosexuality became an accepted way of life in this society and was being publicized as "gay rights," that AIDS became recognizable and manifested in disease.

What is the solution? The solution that is being proposed is "protection." The only way you can prevent AIDS is that you have to have "protection" when you engage in sex. The crime for Magic Johnson was not that he engaged in illegal sex or had sex parties, but that he did not have "protection" available when he did so. So you see, "prophylactics" are being advertised on billboards, on television, being dispensed in the schools and in clinics and they will soon be available next to candy and cigarette machines. But is it going to work? No, it will not work because of several reasons.

1. "Prophylactics" are expensive. A good type costs about one dollar a piece and a drug addict or a teenager will spend that dollar or the number of dollars he may use in one night on drugs or candies rather than on the protection. So it has to be freely available to as many people and as much as they want in order to make any dent.

Another point is the FDA study says that 1 out of 5 condoms have failed the test to hold back the AIDS virus. That is because the AIDS virus is 1/5th the size of sperm and, therefore, is permeable. Now the CDC, which is the Center for Disease Control, is coming up with new guidelines and they are telling people to ask their sex partners some questions before engaging in sex. These are:

1. Have you ever been tested for HIV or other STD?

2. How many sex partners do you have?

3. Have you ever been with a prostitute?

4. For a woman to ask the man, "Have you ever had sex with another man?"

5. Have you ever had sex partners injected with drugs?

6. Have you ever had blood transfusions with blood products?

It becomes clear that if one asks so many questions of his or her sex partner, that person will not agree to have sex with them. They are also coming up with some new advice.

1. Don't do it—that is what we have been telling them, that is to say, abstinence may be unrealistic, but that is the only sure thing.

2. Wear protection

3. Use spermicide

4. Be monogamous. That means "don't fool around." That is what we have been told, too.

5. Avoid anal sex. God has said that too.

But is all of this education changing our lifestyle? Not really. In one survey, the question was asked that as a result of Magic Johnson's announcement that he has AIDS, do you practice safe sex now? 25% said no. Do you talk to your children about AIDS? 27-% said no. Do you limit the number of sex partners you have? 33-% said no. Have you had your blood tested to find out if you are infected?, 57 % said no. Do you contribute to AIDS charities? 59 % said yes because by so giving charity to AIDS they hoped to prevent themselves from getting it..

One of the good things that has happened with the AIDS epidemic is that it has taken care of the sexual revolution of the sixties. People are more careful in engaging in extra-marital sex and choosing their sex partner. As someone at St. Andrew's Church said in 1778, "Fear of disease is a happy restraint to the human being's vain desires, for if human beings were more healthy, there is a chance they will be less righteous." As far as Muslims are concerned, it is not only the fear of disease, but the fear of God's displeasure, as well.

Treatment of women is another social problem in this society. While we Muslims are being blamed for being oppressive to women, keeping them under the veil, making them walk behind us, not giving them their freedom and liberty, and beating them, it is these Jews and Christians who are actually abusing women. When Islam gave women 1,400 years ago the right to divorce, what was the status of women in Europe? When did they get the right to divorce? In America, when did women get the right to vote? (It was is 1921) In New Zealand, women got the right to vote in 1961.

Over 1 million women in this country are abused physically by their husbands or boyfriends to the extent that they have to seek medical help in emergency rooms. Many of them actually end up dying. Now I am not saying that Muslim women are not being abused. They are being abused by Muslim men who do not realize what God has told them and what the Prophet has shown them by example—how to relate to women. Therefore, violence is a problem and it is getting worse also in Muslim communities, but obviously not to the same extent. Therefore, we have to treat our women in a nice way. Prophet has said that, "The best among you is the one who is the best towards his (wife, sister, mother, daughter). We are to provide for them, care for them, and to protect them, not to abuse them verbally, emotionally, and/or physically.

Child abuse is another problem in this country. About 1.7 million reports of child abuse takes place in this country per year out of which 53 % are confirmed. The types of abuse are in these 1992 statistics—400,000 for neglect, 227,000 physical abuse, 138,000 sexual abuse, 57,000 emotional abuse, and 68,000 of other types of abuse.

A Case Against Pornography

Prophet Muhammad (ﷺ) has said about usury, "A time will come when usury will reach the people like 'musk' (perfume)." That is to say, "It will reach everyone whether they want it or not." In the same way, to some extent, nudity and pornography affects all of us whether we want it or not. Just turn on the TV to watch the evening news and you will be confronted with a young woman in a bikini to advertise for one-calorie Pepsi or for feminine hygiene products or for nutritious cereal. If you want some more action, you can watch the soap operas or prime time programs like "Full House" or late night movies. It reaches also in the written media, in magazines, newspapers and in music programs like MTV and Friday night video, etc.

It is not enough to say to Muslim youth that Islam prohibits such things. They ask for the reasoning process behind why it is wrong, what it leads to and so forth. They will not accept, "Don't watch it," when they ask, "Why?" and the answer comes back, "Because I said so." They ask to discuss the pros and cons to arrive at an intelligent answer. The proponents of nudity present the following argument:

1. It is protected by freedom of speech. The response is that the First Amendment is misunderstood and misapplied. Yes, we have certain rights and certain freedoms, but there is a concept of limited freedom. As long as my freedom does not affect someone else's freedom, it may be okay. If I smoke in my own closet, dance naked in my own bedroom, I am affecting only myself, but if I do the same thing outside, I am encroaching on the freedom of other people. Just like we do not like to get second-hand smoke, we don't have to accept second-hand nudity and pornography. Therefore, this is a wrong definition of freedom of expression.

2. It is harmless entertainment as compared to the violence in TV and movies. Response: True, in the short term, nudity and pornography appear to be less harmful than the violence shown on TV and in the movies. However, the long-term effect in much more serious and sometimes the two are tied together. It is a form of an addiction. Ted Bundy, the serial killer, admitted that his criminal behavior began by watching movies on bondage and pornography. Child pornography is another disease which has contributed to 500,000 cases of incest involving father and daughter per year in this country. Child slave trade for sex involves 5 million children worldwide.

3. It is educational. Response: If at all true, it is a poor quality of education. Most of the lessons on anatomy are given to medical students these days on a calendar or a plastic replica. It is not necessary to show live human bodies and sex ads to impart education. Even sex education,as such, is more of a theory than practice. How can a person receiving such a vivid education refrain himself from practicing on others? This is the reason for more than 100,000 rapes being committed annually in this country and the majority of date rapes are not even reported. How can bondage be called "education." Positions of sex can be learned after marriage by experiment rather than by memorizing books or movies?

If it is not necessary to teach baby ducks how to swim, why is it necessary for teenagers to be taught the education of sexual techniques before they are expected to engage in them.

HARMFUL EFFECTS OF NUDITY AND PORNOGRAPHY

1. Degradation of women. Women and their skin are being used to advertise every product, cosmetics, dresses, perfumes and even medications. It is a form of oppression of women and a form of enslaving them. Many of the exercise videos are using obscene positions to sell those programs. Many of the unnatural sex acts shown in some of the x-rated movies are committed by force and under threat. Many of the tortures which are shown in bondage are against the will of women.

2. Watching nudity desensitizes men and women to normal sexual stimulus. People get used to it and therefore, this is the most common cause of psychological impotency in this country. Just by becoming used to these in order to get an arousal, they have to perform some more weird acts than plain, simple nudity can provide.

3. Nudity and pornography are an addiction which leads to other crimes including drugs, murder, rape, abduction, child molestation, and incest. One leads to another until a person pays for that crime behind bars for many years to come. It is not as innocuous as people claim. It is a perversion. There are clubs of sex alcoholics just like Alcoholics Anonymous or AA where people share their previous experiences in order to enter therapy.

4. Finally, it is a waste of time. The time that is spent on vain desires and pursuit of happiness at the cost of others can be utilized in many constructive ways to include improving their knowledge by reading good books, doing housework, sports, exercise or perhaps of remembrance of God because to Him is our return.

Islam blocks the wrong act at its inception and not at the end. Not only is the drinking of wine prohibited, but selling it, serving it, keeping it, or even growing grapes just for the purpose of selling it to a winery is also prohibited. In the same context, not only premarital and extra-marital sex is prohibited, but anything which leads to such, that is, the close intimate mixing of two sexes is also prohibited. Thus the concept of "do not come near adultery" given in the Holy Quran is better than "thou shall not commit adultery," mentioned in the Bible. In the latter phase, it is impolite or wrongful that you go ahead and do anything that can lead up to adultery as long as you do not commit the act itself, while in the former, anything which leads to adultery is also wrong.

Thus, in Islam there is the concept of lowering the gaze for both women and men when they look at each other because it is through visual stimulation that other thoughts take place and hormones come into action which incline people to do things which they would otherwise not do.

There is also a concept of modesty (*hiya*) which is a beautiful characteristic of a true believer. Modesty is maintained by keeping his or her gaze low and trying to protect himself or herself from wrongful influences. The incentive to do right is more if we know the consequences of doing wrong in this life and in the life hereafter.

Now I want to comment about the tools of survival. The tools of social survival for us are: 1) development of our physical well-being.,That is, to take care of our health; 2) our moral and spiritual well-being; 3) educational well-being; 4) to practice Islam collectively; 5) to gain financial strength; 6) political strength; 7) sharing our blessings; 8) unity for the sake of God's satisfaction.

Now let me give you the guiding principles from the Holy Quran for the tools of survival. For the matters of health, we are told, "*We created the human being in the best of them all but then we restored him to the lowest of the low except for those who believe and do good*" (95:4-5). Good health from God is a gift to us and our body is a trust from Him. Not taking care of our bodies is a breach of trust for which we will be held accountable.

Second, "*Blessed is He in whose hand is the sovereignty and He is able to do all things who created life and death that He may test you, which of you is in best conduct and He is the mighty, the forgiving*" (67:1-3). Again, this verse tells us that we are here on this earth as a result of a design of God that we conduct ourselves in a manner that we were told to conduct and then we give this account on how we conducted ourselves in a test when we appear before Him once again.

Third,,"*Successful are the ones who purify themselves and losers are the ones who pollute their souls*" (91:7-9). This verse stresses the importance of chastity and purity of conduct. We need to instill this concept in all of us, especially our youth who are more prone to temptations of the world.

The fourth principle is the abomination for adultery. "*Do not come near to adultery. Surely it is a shameful deed and evil opening roads to other evil."* (17:32). What this means is that the approach or whatever leads to adultery should also be blocked. When the Bible says, "Thou shall not commit adultery," people take it the wrong way thinking that you can do anything which may lead to adultery, but stop short of committing adultery. Islam not only forbids that wrong at the end, but also at the inception. Thus, social mixing or wearing provocative clothes or many other forms, like drinking alcohol which can lead to adultery between men and women, are also prohibited.

Premarital sex which leads to the problems mentioned earlier including abortion, is nothing but to sustain a way of life free from any patience. As one of the Western scholars has said, "Without God, everything is possible." So most of the 1.2 million abortions which are done in this country are not to save the life of the mother or for the sake of rape or incest but to sustain a life of sexual freedom. What does God say in the Holy Quran for those who want to have such enjoyment? *"Such as those who took their way of life to be more amusement and play and were deceived by life of this world, that we shall forget them as they forgot the meeting of this date of theirs and they were bent upon rejecting Our Signs"* (7:51).

In order to attain Islamic education, we have to emphasize the value of total education. If we are going to leave our children 40 hours a week in secular schools, we cannot compete with 2 hours of religious education in Sunday school. Thus, we have to put forth equal efforts. In Islamic school, not only do we need to teach the Quran and religious knowledge, but also how to conduct ourselves in the outside world, especially in dealing with the opposite sex and combatting peer pressure.

I am proposing that Islamic schools should develop curriculum for gender interaction or sex education with a course being given to girls by female physicians and nurses or teachers and to the boys by male physicians or other elders to prepare them for a life which they will be living once they reach puberty and get married. We have also a need to bring Muslim boys and girls together under Islamic guidelines in knowing each other so that when they do decide to marry, they choose a Muslim counterpart. Muslim youth have told me, "Our parents do not allow us to see a person of the opposite sex except in the mosques and at Sunday school, but they do not control us in seeing or meeting the opposite sex of non-Muslims in a school system." Now who do you think they will marry when they grow up? The one with whom they have spent 8 hours a day,

5 days a week, or the one whom they are never allowed to meet and see or talk to.

We have to teach our men that women are not just a bed partner or a housekeeper. We are told in Quran to treat them with respect. In the chapter on women the Quran starts by saying, *"Oh people, keep your duty to your Lord who created you from a single being and created its mate of the same kind and spirit; from these two, many men and women and keep your duty to God by whom you demand one other your rights and to the ties of relationship surely God is ever watching you"* (4:1). So we are to respect the woman who gave birth to us, who kept us in their body for nine months and nurtured us before we were ever able to stand on our feet. And Prophet Muhammad (ﷺ) has said that "the importance of mother in one who is going to lead you to paradise, is three times more than that of the father."

The verse which deals with the relationship of husband and wife says, *"Women are garment for men and men are garment for women"* (2:187). What does that mean that since clothes protect us from outside influences of weather since they are close to our body, since they beautify us, since they are available to us all the time, so should be role of our spouse in our life. Islam places great emphasis on marriage as an institution. It says, "Among his signs is this that He created for you mates from among yourself that you many dwell in tranquility with them and He has put love and mercy between your heart. Thus in that are signs for those who reflect" (30:21). And our beloved Prophet has said that "marriage is my tradition. He who rejects my tradition is not one of us." (see Bukhari and Muslim) He also said, "Marriage is half of the religion, the other half is being God-fearing" (see Tabarani and Hakim).

In terms of AIDS education, we have to take precautions in being exposed to contaminated blood and secretions if we are in a medical profession or we are a patient. Many people are having auto-transfusion, that is, using their own blood, before an elective surgery or doing emergency requesting blood from their relatives.

We are also to teach our non-Muslim friends how homosexuality has been condemned in all the scripture and they have to return to basic teachings if they have to deal with the problem on a permanent basis.

In a community center, we have to work toward establishing clinics for taking care of Muslims who are not able to afford private medical care. We need to also give training to our people for paramedical help and we need to do public education in such clinics. The training of paramedical people should involve first-aid and nursing, CPR, pre-school physical, nutritional counseling, psychological counseling and taking care of sports injuries. We also need to develop a program for exercise for Muslim men and women.

I suggest that in each community center, there should be an exercise room and days can be assigned that Muslim men and women or boys and girls can enjoy it on separate days. We need to teach our community to quit smoking, to manage their stress, their weight and recognize warning symptoms for chronic diseases like diabetes, high blood pressure and heart disease and maybe we can have a screening program for them, too. We also need to take care of our Muslim inmates in the prisons As you know, there are 200,000 Muslims in the U.S. prisons now. They were not Muslims when they entered the prisons. They were sentenced to prison in an anonymous state and by the Grace of God, they are coming out as Muslims including Mike Tyson. Do we have a program for them when they come out so that they will be absorbed by the Muslim community? Will Muslim women or men be likely to marry them? Will Muslim employers give them a job so that they do not need to commit another crime and end up in jail again as ,many of the other inmates do? These are some questions that we have to think about. I am proposing that in each community center, there should be a social support committee which should consist of the Imam, the Muslim physicians, Muslim attorney, a nurse, a psychologist, a counselor who is able to provide for the social needs of the community either in terms of care or advise of counseling and crisis.

Finally the Quran says, *"You have been created as best of the mankind because you enjoin what is good and forbid what is wrong and you believe in God"* (3:110). Is one of our purpose of life but remember, this verse is not a blank check that we have been raised as best community unless we do those three things and this verse also tells us that there is no concept in Islam of secular humanism or being a nice guy unless we do something as a believer for God's satisfaction.

4 MARITAL RELATIONS AND MUTUAL RIGHTS IN ISLAM

66*Believers, men and women, are protectors of one another. They enjoin what is just and forbid what is evil. They observe regular prayer and practice regular charity, obey God and His messenger, and on them God will pour His mercy, for God is exalted in power and right. God has promised to believers, men and women, gardens under which we were supposed to dwell therein, beautiful mansions and garden of everlasting bliss, for the greatest bliss is the pleasure of God, that is the supreme"* (9:71).

We are told in the Quran that, *"Men and women believers are protectors of each other."* We are also told in the Quran that our spouses have been created for us for our own benefit so that we enjoy tranquility. It is said in the Quran, *"All you believe, observe your duty to your Lord who created you from a single being and created its mate of the same kind and expect from this too many men and women and keep your duty to God by whom you demand of one another's right and the ties of relationship surely God is every watching over you"* (4:1).

And we are also told, *"And one of His signs that He created for you, your mate from among yourselves that you may dwell in tranquility with them and He has put love and mercy between your hearts verily in that are the signs for those who reflect"* (30:21).

Prophet Muhammad (ص) has told us how we should treat our spouse. It was an important part of his last sermon and he states, "Oh, you peo-

29

ple, your wives have a certain right over you and you have certain rights over them. Treat them well and be kind to them for they are your committed partners and helpers." Whatever he said was an inspiration from God. Whatever he said, we can confirm the authenticity of that by going back to the Quran and see what the Quran says on this subject.

It says, *"Provide for them, the rich according to his income and the poor according to his means, the provision according to the custom, this is an obligation for those who act kindly"* (2:236). So providing for them according to your means is an obligation.

And God also says, *"Treat them politely for even if you dislike them, perhaps you dislike something which God has placed much good"* (4:19). So there may be some reasons why you may not like your spouse for any physical or other reasons, but we are told still to like them because God has chosen them for us.

Prophet Muhammad (ﷺ) has expressed some of the rights of wives on their husbands or the instructions to husbands for their wives. In *Mishkat*, it is reported the best and the most perfect of the believers is the one who is superior in his moral behavior and kind and courteous to his wife. In another place, he has said, "Feed her when you feed yourself, clad her when you provide yourself with cloth, neither hit her on the face nor use impolite language" (see Tirmidhi).

In Abu Daud, he is reported to have said, "When a man wakes up his wife and both of them perform two cycles of prescribed prayer together, the name of the husband is recorded among those who remember God and the name of the wife is recorded among those who remember." But he was fair and he has also outlined the duties and responsibilities of the wife towards her husband. I will just mention three of them here from his collection of Traditions. In this part of Tirmidhi, it is reported that he said, "A woman who prays five times a day, fasts during the month of Ramadan, protects her modesty and is obedient to her husband may enter heaven through any door she likes." Not only can she enter heaven, but she can choose from the different doors. In another Tradition, it is mentioned, "The best woman is the one who greets her husband with joy when he looks at her and when he asks something lawful, she obeys and never adopts any attitude in connection with her own self and good which is disliked by him." In another Tradition, it is reported,"On the Day of Judgment, God will not look upon the woman who has been ungrateful to her husband."

There have been many, many women in Islam who were great leaders, prophet's wives, Khadija and Ayisha and many others such as the Prophet's daughter, Fatima, the leader of the women in heaven. There have been many known scholars who have been women. Imam Malik's teacher, Ayisha, daughter of Sa'd ibn Waqqas, Imam Shafi'i"s teacher was Saiyida Nafisa, granddaughter of Imam Hasan, Rabia Basri, another scholar of Islam, was such a great scholar that men scholars used to come and study with her. Even nowadays, there have been scholars like Zaynab Ghazali. Women can achieve their rights if they are given the opportunity to do so. They need to know that they do not have to stay in the house and cook and take care of the children,

In my opinion, God has also been kinder to women. First of all, they are equal to men in all acts of piety. The Quran assures this (see 33:35). For example, when men miss their prescribed prayers, they are religiously obligated to make up for them. However, when women miss their prescribed prayers because of certain days of the month, they are not required to make them up. Men must provide for their wives, whether their wives work outside the home or not. If women earn income, it belongs to them alone and they can spend it on themselves if they want. They do not have to provide to their husband from that income.

Now let's look briefly at women's rights according to modern society. The women's lib movement, in my opinion, is distorted. In this movement, women have rights, as I described, to do the right thing, but they also have the right to compete in wrongdoings. Not wearing the modest dress is not a question of women's rights, having an abortion is not a question of a women's rights. Cancer of the lungs was the 10th leading cause of death in women fifty years ago when they were not competing with men in smoking; Now it is the second leading cause of death in them, thanks to their "liberation."

God says in the Quran *"Oh, humanity, it is you who is needy of God, and it is God who is above all needs"* (35:15). So the question of rights should be taken in the sense of who is the giver of rights, to whom are we responsible for having given us these rights. It is God Who had given us these rights. We must accept our responsibilities when we talk about our rights.

The relationship between husband and wife has been summarized in one beautiful sentence in Quran which should be the guiding light, *"They are your garments and you are their garments"* (2:187). Only He knows why He used the word "garment." We can only guess. A garment is close to our body. So husband and wife should remain close to each other. A garment protects our body from outside influences; thus husband and wife should protect each other from outside temptation. A garment is to beautify our appearance so they should complement each other and not belittle each other. A garment is always available to our body, so should they be to each other.

The following verse is frequently quoted by men, but is misunderstood very much. *"Men are protector of women because God has made them excel over the other, and because they spend their property on women, so good women are obedient (to their husband) and guard their modesty. As for whom you fear rebellion, admonish them, and then banish them from your bed (i.e., do not sleep with them), or beat them (lightly). If they obey you, then seek not a way against them, God is ever High and Exalted"* (4:34)

Wife abuse is a major social crime in American society. Close to 4million women are physically abused every year by their husbands, ex-husbands, or boyfriends to the extent of seeking medical attention in emergency rooms according to a 1991 Senate report. Many such abuses are not reported by women for the fear of divorce or further abuse. About three women die every year from such abuse. Abuse is not only physical but also sometime sexual (rape), emotional, or financial.

Unless Muslims guard themselves to prevent such social crimes, they will become (and are becoming) a part of our own society, just as divorce has become. Muslim women are much less likely to report abuse and to whom will they report? to the male Imam? Do we have a social support agency or should they call non-Muslim law enforcement agencies and have their bread earners imprisoned? The mention of "beat them lightly" in the Quran is not for all women, but only those women who are rebellious (disloyal) and in stages 1) first you warn them; 2) you separate your bed from them; 3) beat them lightly (with a traditional "toothbrush" or folded handkerchief) before the final stage; 4) divorce, one of the most-hated permissions. The Prophet himself did not beat any of his wives and told Muslims, "Do not beat God's handmaidens," and "How could they beat their women in daytime as slaves and then sleep with them in the night?"

Talking about women's status in Islam is easy. To give them their due rights in practice is difficult. The process can begin by giving them 1) equal say in the decision-making process in the home whether it is weaning of infant or education of growing children or financial matters; 2) full opportunity to learn Islam as well as "secular" education so that they can help their children learn since the first school is at home; 3) acquire skills to help the Muslim community whether in education, nursing, or professions in the less male contact areas; and 4) involve them in the operation and decision-making process in Muslim organizations and even in Mosques. It is unfortunate and contrary to the teachings of Prophet Muhammad (ﷺ) that Muslim women are not encouraged to pray in mosques in Muslim countries.

My advice to married couples for a happy marriage is no different than the advise given to them by many counselors.

1. I suggest that both of them be conscious of their personal appearance and try to remain attractive to each other. It is not uncommon that women dress and put on make-up when they go out, but don't do the same when they are inside to please their husbands. Similarly, when men want their wives to be very attractive-looking, they should also look at their own appearance and especially their physical appearance so that they will be pleasing to their wives. Both of them live in a society in which there are too many temptations outside the home and, therefore, they should not give any chance to others to succumb to such temptations.

2. I suggest both of them be companions to each other rather than the role of the boss and the one who is being bossed or upper-hand or lower-hand. If the two wheels of a vehicle are of the same diameter, same air pressure, then the car will go in a straight line, otherwise it will not. So, I suggest they be each other's friend more than being their bed partner.

3. When they do commit mistakes or injustice to each other, they should admit it and be forgiven. They should be gentle in criticism and generous in appreciation. They should never bring up their past because it is like undoing the dressing and starting the wound fresh.

4. They should mind their language. Sometimes we say things which we don't mean but it hurts other people. As the poet says, "The wounds of blade many heal one day, but the wounds of tongue never heal." So before we says something, we should think how these words will affect the other person or if we are the recipient of those words, how we would feel.

5. They should have a sense of humor. One woman describes her husband in this way, that many men had proposed to me and they liked me, but I chose him as my mate for the rest of my life because he makes me laugh all the time. Life is too short to be too serious. If we have a smile

for each other when we greet each other and a word of kindness and of compassion, it has a lasting effect. Again the poet says, "The sweet words of kindness and sweet words of love make this world happy like heaven above."

6. Both of them should share household duties together. It is not fair that women are used as a cook and as a maid and as a babysitter while men enjoy all outdoor and outside of the home social activities. The Prophet (ﺹ), always helped his wife in household work and he was an example for us.

7. They should find occasions to give each other a gift or flowers or candy, whatever a small thing that may be. This is not a western concept. In fact, the Prophet has stressed that we should give gifts to each other because "giving gifts" increases mutual love.

8. Wives should recognize the economic means of their husbands and should not put any demand on him that he cannot bear. If they do, he will either refuse or find wrong means to earn extra income to meet her demands and both of which will have wrong results.

9. They should be equally involved in community work and efforts. It is not appropriate that mothers have to bring children for Sunday school while fathers stay home to watch football games. If learning Islam is good for children, it is good for mothers and it is also good for fathers.

10. In matters of sex, both them should be available to each other without putting an extra burden on either one. Thus, the Prophet (ﺹ), was a very modern man. He encouraged foreplay. In a Tradition, he has said, "It is not appropriate that you fall upon your wives like a beast but you must send a message of love beforehand." Men and women both have physiological desires. Each should respect the likes and dislikes of each other. We should respect each others privacy because each of us needs some time, moments of privacy, to be alone with our body or with our mind.

11. Finally, they should have meals together and the occasions for meals should be happy occasions for the whole family and not a time for arguments. If they are going to argue, they should do so later on and not in front of their children but separately. Each argument should end with some expression of love. It is recommended that they should never go to bed mad at each other. If we respect each other the same way we like to be respected, it will increase our trust and love and hopefully, we will realize that God, who has promised to put love in our heart, has done it.

5 INFLUENCING THE BEHAVIOR OF MUSLIM YOUTH AND THEIR PARENTS

The purpose of this article is to evaluate the factors influencing the behavior of children and how to modify them so that they grow as model citizens practicing Islam in their community, become a source of joy and comfort to their parents, and maintain family harmony.

The behavior of growing children is influenced by many factors that include their parents and other close relatives, teachers, peers at school, community and the media. Lack of discipline and civilized behavior at school is a major problem in the U.S., the fallout of which is also seen at home! With broken families and the absence of a father at home, this becomes a major problem for single mothers raising a teenager.

Muslim children, although distinct in their value system, still are exposed to and affected by what they see and learn. In Islamic teachings, great emphasis has been placed on moral conduct and behavior. The Quran says, *"Lo, the noblest of you, in the sight of God, is (the one) best in conduct. Lo, God is knower, Aware"* (49:13). *"By the soul, and the proportion and order given to it, and its enlightenment as to its wrong, and its right. Truly he succeeds that purifies it (the soul), and he fails that corrupts it"* (91:7-10).

Prophet Muhammad (ص), has said, "I have been sent to perfect your conduct" (Bukhari and Muslim). "A fathers' teaching his child good manners is better than giving a bushel of grain (in charity)" (Bukhari).

Children are very susceptible to any and every influence. It has been

35

said, "They are like molten cement. Anything that falls on them makes a lasting impression." Their minds are like virgin soil, ready to accept any seed. As they grow, their organs of reception start working and accept new ideas and influences. It is up to us to screen the experiential factors that influence a child's development so that they can learn to accept the right ideas and behaviors and reject the wrong influences.

The parents (and close relatives living with them like uncles and grandparents) have only 25% influence in a 6-16 year old child. 50% is by peers at school or in the community. 25% is from the teachers and other sources of education outside home i.e. media, mainly TV (and magazines for older youths). The influence of parents is high during early age (0-8 years, up to 80%), but as the child discovers new friends and ideas, he or she grows independent from the influence of parents.

THE AMERICAN SCENE

The American scene of the behavior of children and adults is changing. While it is difficult to qualify the behavior at home, the same at school has been published. What is happening in our homes is reflective of what's happening outside homes and vice versa According to a study conducted by Fullerton California Police Department of Education,[1] the leading school discipline problem in 1940 was talking, chewing gum, making noise, running in the hallways, getting out of place in line, wearing improper clothing and not putting paper in the wastebasket, etc. In 1980 the major problems were drug abuse, alcohol abuse, pregnancy, suicide, rape, robbery, assault, burglary, arson, and bombing. The Indianapolis public schools conducted a behavior discipline survey.[2] It reported the following activities in the hall: Grabbing 69%, pushing 84%, hitting 82%, kicking 48%, slapping 57%, pinching 66%, fighting 78% and tripping 62%. There is also a high percentage of physical violence by teacher against student (22%) and by student against teacher (42%). We leave our children at school in such an environment for 30-40 hours per week and then expect them to develop into angels.

While the parents can do little to affect other influences, some suggestions can be made in this regard.

PEERS

Keep children in the company of good Muslim children after school and during weekends to dilute the unavoidable influence of undesirable elements at school.

SCHOOL

Choose a school in a good location (neighborhood) irrespective of it being private or public. Get to know the teachers personally and interact with them. Only the neglected children create wrong impression at school and expose themselves to various abuses. Supervise their homework.

MEDIA

Watch TV with your children, and select good educational and entertainment programs. Comment on the negative aspects of the program. Cut down the TV hour to less than 1 1/2 hours on weekdays and 2 1/2 hours on weekends. Do not buy rock music tapes (out of love for your child) nor allow him/her to listen to any hard rock. Encourage outdoor activity in preference to indoor (e.g. TV/music). Encourage them to read newspapers, good magazines (National Geographic) and Islamic periodicals.

ROLE OF PARENTS IN INFLUENCING
THE BEHAVIOR OF THEIR CHILDREN

As I have said many times, "Children will become what we want them to be if we are what we want them to be." Children cannot be expected to practice Islam by sending them to Sunday school if we are not doing that ourselves in our day to day life. If we want them to get up early in the morning to perform the prescribed prayer, we have to do it ourselves and ask them to join us. If we want them to read the Quran, we should read with them and so on.

LOVE

Growing children may not take an order, but will do things out of love and respect for their parents. So love and respect on a mutual basis is our best weapon against all the negative influences on them. Parental love should be unconditional and on biological grounds rather than on their achievements at school or in sports. Love should not be confused with unlimited permissiveness or with closed eyes towards a child's faults.

Criticizing certain faults of the child should not diminish the love by the parents.

INFORMATION

Children are not born knowing everything right or wrong in social norms. They need clear guidelines about good and bad behavior, Islamic and un-Islamic way of life. The greatest effect is of the parent's attitude and example rather than the words in a book. If children see their parents not practicing what they themselves are told to practice they become rebellious and non-believers (in the value system). A typical example is of alcoholism in the American scene. Children are told it is bad for you until you are 18, while it is not bad for the parents. Therefore children seeing this as hypocrisy, rebel and get alcohol, not from a liquor store, but from their own home or from a friend at parties. Therefore, parents should set the same standards for themselves as they set for their children, and share with them information of all kinds whether related to the outside world or inside the family. It is not the knowledge which hurts, but the lack of it or misuse of it which causes problems.

DECISIONS

Parents should help children make appropriate decisions and be responsible for their decisions. Younger children can only make decisions about the present (i.e. what clothes to wear that day), but grown-ups can make decisions that may affect their future, under parental guidance (i.e. selection of career, school and hobbies). Children left to grow on their own, will regret a lack of direction they had in their childhood. Children should be taught how to be responsible by being given the chance to share household work, keep their desk and room clean and how to handle their "own" money. Let them spend all their money and suffer from the lack of it. A sense of deprivation once in awhile is good for them as long as the reason for deprivation is explained well.

PROBLEMS WITH THE PARENTS

1. If the parents are authoritarian, the child becomes fearful of making mistakes, starts lying for the fear of being punished and feels insecure. Unfortunately, abused children become abusers when they grow up. The parent should remember that the only absolute authority in the house is the Will of God, and everyone has to submit to His Will, in order to

expect submission from a younger person.

2. If the parents are emotionally disturbed and depressed themselves they will not have time for the children, leading them to withdraw, become depressed or develop anti-social activities.

3. If the parents are perfectionists and expect the child to be perfect all the time, the child will have two options. Either he or she will live up to the expectations, or will develop opposite tendencies, i.e. a teenager keeping his or her room messy to get back at the "ever cleaning" mom. Parents should not make "all" the choices for their children, but help in their individual growth.

4. The over-protective, anxious parent cannot raise a confident child ready to deal with the real life. This child will feel danger everywhere. While the child has to be supervised, he or she does not need the physical presence of the parent at all time. They should raise a strong child, strong enough to carry on their work if they meet a sudden death themselves.

5. The parent who cannot say no to a child, spoils him or her by providing him or her with every wish every time. This child will demand whatever he or she wants immediately and put on a manipulative show to get it. One parent complained how their five year old will stop breathing until she got what she wanted. The parents have to learn to control their love and discipline themselves in order to discipline their children The child's necessary desires should be met according to the means of the family, but a time may come when a firm no should be put into practice.

6. Parents who take sides in sibling rivalry encourage jealousy and hate. They should not prefer boys over girls or the reverse and fair complexion over dark ones, bright ones over less bright, but try to be fair to all of them and neutral in their fights.

HOW PARENTS CAN COMMUNICATE
WITH THEIR CHILDREN

Neither party can influence the other unless they communicate. This is a serious problem in American families. One father told me that at best all his teenage daughter would say to him would be "Hi" one or two times a day. This can be substituted by a "peace be upon you," (*as-salam alaykum*) in a Muslim family in which parents and teenagers are not getting along well. One should avoid getting into this stage of strained communication.

1. Find a time and place to talk to your children. Children are sometimes in a "bad mood" upon returning from school, loaded with homework, as are parents in the afternoon with a busy day at work. The best time to have a chat is during breakfast and evening dinner together. Better than this is allotting ten minutes after either the evening or night prescribed prayer or even better, after the dawn prescribed prayer, if time permits. During this session, the parent can inform the children of all the good things they did that day and ask the children the same and share their problems.

2. When you do argue, do it patiently, one person speaking at a time. Be specific and separate emotions from facts. Speak in a low voice. Screaming decreases the intake of the message. Finding fault may make you look like a winner, but remember, just as we want God to forget and forgive our faults, we should do the same for others.

3. Practice active listening to each other's view, even if you don't agree. For religious issues consult the Quran or the Traditions together, rather than quoting from your memory.

4. Refrain from sarcasm, name calling, humiliation, pointing your finger, etc. Read God's injunction about these again and again in Surah Al-Hujurat (49th Surah).

5. Encourage each other even in areas of shortcomings,, rather than making fun or making a negative remark. If your child brings a B report, then instead of, "I doubt you will ever improve or pass your exam," say "A 'B' is better than a 'C', and I am sure you are talented enough to do better. Perhaps I can help you in the areas that you have difficulties at school?"

INFLUENCING THE BEHAVIOR THROUGH DAILY HOUSEHOLD CHORES

The purpose of giving them some chores, is to keep them busy as well as teach them some responsibility. Initially it may be boring, but it will eventually become routine. The assignment should be according to age (and not the sex of the child) and should include setting the table to begin with, then washing dishes, laundry, taking out the garbage or just helping in the garden. However, children should not be forced into doing things, otherwise they will rebel. By the same token, they should not be penalized for mistakes. The best payment for a job is a smile, hug, thank you or praising the child to others, rather than money. While it may be all right to give an allowance, it should not be tied to the job. Otherwise the child will want money for everything. An eleven year old told his mom, "You need to know only three things about kids. Don't hit them too much, don't yell at them too much, and don't do too much for them."

HOW ABOUT INFANTS AND PRE-SCHOOLERS

While studies mainly refer to children ages 6-16 years, the small ones should not be neglected. In fact, in the first year of life, it is the behavior of the parent (especially the mother) which is so crucial and has nearly 90 percent influence. Then, as the child grows, identification with the parent of the same sex may make the influence of that parent more important. The boys watch their father more closely doing mechanical work and girls observe moms carefully doing household work. Sometimes it may be reversed. It is at this time that parents can inject love and respect into children by their example of mutual love and respect for each other and for the children. It is also at this age that doing things together including playing, watching TV, reading, etc. will help establish the foundations (trust, self-confidence, ability, etc.) of open communication. In terms of practice of religion, it comes from observing their parents and doing the practices together. If nice manners are programmed into them before they are introduced to the general population, it is doubtful they would get the infection of misbehavior.

BILL OF RIGHTS FOR MUSLIM CHILDREN

1. Muslim children have the right to learn and practice Islam even if one of their parents is a non-Muslim, or non-practicing Muslim.

2. They have a right to be treated as a person, in an environment that is conducive to their growth and maturity and to become useful citizens.

3. They have a right to receive love, care, discipline, and protection from their parents.

4. They have a right to receive education, and financial protection for the future.

BILL OF RIGHTS FOR MUSLIM PARENTS

1. Parents have a right to receive love, respect and affection from their children as mentioned in the Quran.

2. Parents have a right to educate and discipline their children as mentioned in the Quran and shown by the example of Prophet Muhammad (ﷺ).

3. Parents have a right to know more about their children, and monitor other influences affecting them.

4. Parents have a right to say no to unusual financial and other demands of children.

Finally, I end this article with a verse from the Quran.

"Your Lord has commanded that you worship none but Him, and that you be kind to your parents. If either or both of them reach old age with you, do not say to them any word of contempt, nor repulse them, but address them in terms of honor, and out of kindness lower to them your wings of submission, and say, 'My Lord, have mercy on them as they cared for me in my childhood'" (17:23-24).

6 FRUSTRATIONS OF A MUSLIM AFTER VISITING A MUSLIM COUNTRY

I cannot resist the temptation to record my observations and express my feelings on visiting Pakistan after an absence of many years. Muslims living in a Muslim country are fully conversant with Islamic teachings and are also aware of the un-Islamic customs and traditions they are following, but they have become so used to them, rather immune to them, so much so that they have accepted them as a way of life. When a Muslim, living in a western country, visits a Muslim country or a native Muslim visits his or her own country, after a lapse of some years, he or she encounters unpleasant surprises and severe disappointment of great variety. I wish my people to share my observations and experiences of my visit to Pakistan after several years of stay in the U.S. Whatever I observed and experienced in my brief visit may not be true for the whole of Pakistan or all other Muslim countries I visited. It I offend anyone, I offer my sincere apologies in advance.

PRACTICE OF RELIGION

I wrote earlier that Muslims living in a non-Muslim country are living in a spiritual and social vacuum. Here, on the surface, Islam is everywhere, on the radio, on the television, in crowded mosques (crowded for Friday prescribed congregational prayer only, vacant other days) and in the newspapers. When one turns on the television, it starts with the recitation of the Holy Quran, commentary, and gives the call to the prescribed prayer at the time of the prescribed prayer (to which few people respond) and it ends with the same. The same is true of other media. Islam is there and obvious in appearance. It is not seen being practiced by the majority in day to day life. In a given family, though everyone listens to the call to the prescribed prayer, few, one or two old people, perform prescribed prayer as if others are exempt from it. Similarly, during Ramadan, mostly old people and some young men keep fast. Many do not keep fast for the fear of becoming weak. Fasting is best that they do in Ramadan. Even when they do it, only few pray daily except for the Friday prescribed congregational prayer. Few people read the Quran on a daily basis.

Talking about the Quran, it can be said that it is considered a sacred book kept on the highest shelf with lots of dust on the cover. No one bothers to consult it for guidance on day to day matters of life, as if it is not a book showing the right way of life. People invite other Muslims to read the Quran in a group upon the occasions of death, birth, and buying a new house just for the purpose of blessings. Only a few of them know the meanings and interpretations of the commands of God Almighty and it has been left to those who have a monopoly on religious knowledge. However, everyone loves to criticize scholars like Maududi, Khomeini, and Syed Qutb without bothering to check with the Quran or Traditions whether the saying or teachings of them are true or not. I believe most Muslims in Muslim countries take being Muslim for granted and feel that they don't have to read the Quran daily, interpret it and follow its teachings in their lives. Some of them may not know or believe that the Quran is the actual words of God and is the source of all knowledge and is a guide for everyone who believes in it and seeks guidance from it. The Quran is the Truth for the present and so it is forever, as it was fourteen hundred years ago.

ISLAMIC LAWS AND THEIR IMPLEMENTATION

Some Islamic laws have been imposed by the government The poor-due (*zakat*) is being collected from saving accounts; since Shias and Qadianis, as well as Christians are exempted, according to a banker friend of mine, people are filling false documents about their religious beliefs. Harsh Islamic punishments exist and are given to offenders on account of adultery, theft, etc. It's done in public or on the streets. If the crimes are committed in the four walls of high society, they are acceptable. Serving alcohol is forbidden to Muslims in public, but not within the four walls of the houses, or in a hotel room. Islamic laws and punishment have not eliminated rape, abduction, theft, and murder. This is not unexpected when the observance of law is forced from above (without practical example) rather than accepted by people themselves. The concept of repentance and piety is not there in the purest form.

In Pakistan, the first known case of heroin addiction was recorded in 1980. In 1981, there were only 25 cases recorded. By 1986, there were half-a-million cases. Now it is estimated that there are between one and one-and-a-half million cases in a population of 95 million. The rate of growth of narcotic addiction in Pakistan is higher than that of the U.S. In addition to heroin addicts, there are about one million opium and hashish users and 300,000 tranquilizer abusers. The actual number of alcoholics is hard to determine, since they usually don't seek treatment. There are only 26 rehabilitation centers and 10,000 trained social workers.

It seems that the Islamic Law is meant for the poor only. The rich and privileged are all above the law. Even at the level of common people, the observance of Islam is forced upon from the top, whether it is being accepted willingly by the people or not. People are made to hear the call to the prescribed prayer on the radio, loudspeaker, and television, and asked to close hotels in Ramadan. A sick person or a foreigner who does not have a home can hardly find a place outside to eat.

OPERATION OF THE GOVERNMENT

One would expect that in an Islamic country where Islamic Law is enforced, that the government would operate on lines somewhat similar to that of the Companion of the Prophet and second rightly-guided caliph, Umar. It is an ideal which could hardly be achieved by modern Muslim rulers. What grieves us is the lack of enthusiasm to emulate <u>him</u>. On the contrary, bribery is to be found on every level. Nothing moves in Pakistan, whether at the airport, customs, offices, or telephone department without bribery. To get work done, you have to give some bribes. in these departments, clerks whose salary is 1500 rupees are actually making 5000 rupees from other sources. Interest is banned but it has been given a new name called, "profit." The poor-due is collected from the saving accounts of the poor, widows, orphans and even old people depending on remittances from their relatives in the Middle East. Very few folks really work in the government offices. Officers reach offices late and after working half an hour, they go for a tea break and then there is lunchtime. They come back at 1:30 for a few minutes and leave at 2:00 again. The peon misbehaves with visitors and takes his tip before giving an appointment with the boss.

PEOPLE'S BEHAVIOR AND MORAL CONDUCT

One would expect that the dealings of peoples among themselves would be according to the commands of God Almighty as given on many instances in the Quran, especially in Surah Al-Hujurat and as shown by the example of the Prophet (ﷺ). To the contrary, rudeness, cheating, telling lies, backbiting, arrogance, ridicule of others, etc., became their second nature and is apparent when they talk, walk, or behave in society. The basic positive moral values and negative moral values are common to all religions. Even non-religious societies appreciate positive values and denounce negative values. Therefore, good virtues are part of human behavior and the lack of them naturally creates doubt in our minds about a person being called a human being in the true sense. So to be a good Muslim, one should be a good human being first.

ACCEPTANCE OF THE LAW

A non-Muslim is accountable to the lawmakers, law-enforcing agencies, and to the state. A Muslim is not only responsible to the above agencies, but also to the Creator, the Ultimate Lawmaker. As a result, a non-Muslim can hide away or try to escape after committing a crime; while, a Muslim knows that there is no escape for him. He will be caught in the hereafter. He cannot escape punishment. Even if no man or woman has seen him committing a crime, God is watching and is aware of it. This fear of God Almighty or piety is the key to the regulation of Muslim's moral code of conduct. The fact that in practice, in Muslim countries, people are showing all abnormal deviant moral character as listed in the beginning, tells me that such offenders of arrogance, falsehood, rudeness, cheating, bribery, theft, and backbiting either are not aware of God's Almighty's Omnipresence, or His commands, or they do not believe in them or they believe that no one is watching them and recording their misdeeds or will take them into account. In a society where Muslims are not practicing Islam, the imposition of Islamic Law is not appropriate. For example, if a person is hungry and is not taken care of either by the state or his neighbors, and if he commits theft to feed his hungry children, cutting off his hand is not appropriate or Islamic, because in a true Islamic welfare state, no one should be allowed to remain hungry and unattended. We have the example of Caliph Umar to follow.

EDUCATION OF CHILDREN AND ADULTS

The importance of education is obvious from the fact that the command of God Almighty to mankind is "recite." *"Recite in the name of God who created you from a mere clot."* On the subject of education and its purpose, there are many verses in the Quran and also in the sayings of the Holy Prophet. They are usually on display on beautiful boards on every corner of the Karachi roads, so I will not reiterate. However, in practice, this is not true. Children read not to seek knowledge but to pass examinations so that they get a job or can get out of Pakistan to the the Middle East for the better job prospects It is the fashion of the day for a young Muslim to either quote, misquote, or denounce Islamic scholars like Maududi, Khomeini, Syed Qutb, and others without checking into facts, without verifying what is true and what is not. Everyone loves to quote and discuss the teachings of Islam, quoting someone else, but his own knowledge and study is negligible. If you take into account whatever little knowledge they have and how far they translate it into their actions, it is nothing at all. The children in a famous television program (Suhail Rana's) seem to be very knowledgeable, but average children that I met knew nothing of Islam as expected of them at their age level. When it comes to practice, say for example, prescribed prayer, mostly old folks offer prescribed prayer five times a day. The knowledge is there but its acceptance and translation into action is not.

ISLAMIC CULTURE

One of my friends, who is a U.S. citizen, recently moved back to Pakistan. When asked why, he said, "It is not for money, since in Pakistan I will be making less money, it is not for religion since I am not a religious person, it is for the sole purpose of my culture which I missed very much in the U.S."

I will try to define what is or what should be an Islamic culture. However, I will just narrate my observations of Pakistani culture. In a given marriage, every night song sessions will start when all the girls of the house, their neighborhood friends and brothers, assemble and start with typical marriage songs which will quickly change to film songs and then to English western songs. Then dancing will start with the boys and girls dancing together to the tune of the Luddi dance and again quickly changing into the Twist and Disco dances. The music is relayed by loud-speakers to the distress of the whole neighborhood until 3:00 a.m.

Similarly, a display of culture in public is fascinating, whether in terms of a public show, a local movie, or a marriage party. Nothing is related to Islamic Law and practices, for example, lighting candles around the bride, throwing money over the couple's head. The highest Islamic practices are kissing and keeping over the head a copy of the Quran. And one friend commented, "If the people are given any book in Arabic, they will even kiss that, and keep it on the highest shelf, since they cannot tell the difference." They hardly open the book or try to read it. Fashion is at its peak. Young girls try to be a model with artificial eye-brows, lipstick, and other foreign cosmetics. Rich housewives spend a couple of hours and several hundred rupees in a beauty parlor before going to a party. Pakistan is one of the poorest countries in the U.N. direc-tory, but it appears a lie if you are attending an upper class wedding party. In an average party estimated women are wearing at least ten million rupees worth of gold. At least forty such parties go on every day and there are many cities.

LOVE AND HATE FOR AMERICA

If one visits any of the so-called non-aligned, underdeveloped nations of Asia, Africa, or Latin America, one will observe that criticizing the policies of the U.S., in the press or in high society gatherings, is the fash-ion of the day. Even the so-called leftists, who never stop shouting against the imperialistic, satanic U.S. and her evil designs, actually practice just the opposite. If American policies are bad and the U.S. is worth hating;, everything which the U.S. makes is in highest demand and is being sought? This applies not only to automobiles, toothpaste, food items, medicines, and machinery, etc., it extends even to copying the American accent and American pop songs and dances. Pakistanis just talk about their hate for America, but in practice, everything that America can pro-duce, promote, or stand for is lovable and indispensable for them. They call America a land of infidels (*kafirs*) There is a lot of alcoholism, drug abuse, violence and pornography in the U.S., but not in American Muslims.

THE LOVE AND HATE FOR THE ARCH ENEMY (INDIA)

Most of today's Pakistani youth do not know how Pakistan was created and how many lives of their ancestors were lost in the struggle for an independent Muslim homeland. To be specific, about one million Muslims of the subcontinent were killed in the Hindu-Muslim-Sikh riots and nearly ten million displaced. But all that is a fact of history now. With the fervor, the Pakistanis love Indian music, Indian movies, Indian dances and clothes and other Indian products, their acceptance of the dominance of Hindu culture is exposed. Through culture and wedding rituals, Hinduism is befriending Pakistani society. Now, how can we ever fight someone whose values are so dear to us? Thus, by allowing India to divide Pakistan into Bangladesh and Pakistan, we have proved that One-Nation theory for Muslims of India was just a dream. It is these linguistic and ethnic ties which have weakened the One-Nation theory. Pathans and Punjabi Muslims who were the Soldiers of Islam in India before 1947 now think of themselves as Soldiers of their province only.

LIVING CONDITIONS AND HEALTH

The descendants of the torch-bearers of the glorious civilizations, when Europe was in the dark ages, are now themselves living in filth and crowded slums, except a few. Transportation is horrible. The people ride in buses hanging by the door (and they sometimes fall off). The rich travel in air-conditioned foreign cars. The access to good medical facilities is the right of the rich. The rich and the influential can get the best care available locally or be taken to the U.K. or the U.S. for better medical treatment. The poor have a choice of whether to accept the minimum offered to them (like an out-dated aspirin) or die on the street or die while waiting in the emergency room of a crowded hospital. What a contrast, and what a concept of Islamic welfare state. Food adulteration is common and is seen at all levels openly. Muslims in the U.S. are concerned if there is lard in certain items; poor Muslims of Pakistan who are (without this knowledge) are made to eat meat of dead cow, buffalo, goat, horse or even dogs, adulterated milk, shortening and spices. Merchants never think that there is someone watching them and who will ask them questions on the Day of Judgment. They believe that doing some charity or worshipping one night in a year, or the recommendation of their Prophet will save them.

CONCLUSION

In brief, if a new Muslim or "born again" Muslim from the West visits a Muslim country, he will be shocked to see the dichotomy and hypocrisy in the preaching and practicing of Islam. So he should keep his expectations low and keep his mouth shut and his eyes closed, and ears plugged; otherwise, he will lose his peace of mind.

7 THE LAWFUL AND THE PROHIBITED: OUR NEED, OUR OBSESSION

"Oh you who believe, make not unlawful the good things which God has made lawful for you, but commit no excess for God loves not those who commit excess" (5:90).

Living as a Muslim in a non-Muslim society is difficult but not impossible. We are to enjoy what is permitted and avoid what is forbidden. Sometimes this distinction is easy and sometimes it is not. There are situations that fall in the grey zone and according to the Traditions we are also to avoid that which is doubtful. However, what is not appropriate is that we like to do things which are wrong because of a cultural habit that we have formed and justified. On the other hand, there are things that we must do: for example, attending Friday prescribed congregational prayer, but we find an excuse not to do so. Thus we should not try to make what is forbidden, permissible and what is permissible, forbidden because it is only up to God to do so. Also sometimes we are not able to define priorities of certain situations. For example, someone may be very careful in choosing the blessed slaughtered meat because that is permissible, but not careful in performing the five daily prescribed prayers which are obligatory. On the Day of Judgment, we will be first questioned about our prescribed prayers much before we will be questioned about what kind of meat we ate.

The late Dr. Fazlur Rahman once wrote an article entitled "How to Revive Islam From the Debris of It's Past." By past, he meant the past

1,300 years because some Muslims have not tried to figure out how Islam flourished and developed after the first one hundred years, especially when they went to non-Muslim societies in Africa, Europe, Asia, and the Far East.

By the debris, he meant all the cultural and regional influences on Islam which have covered the beauty and essence of pure way of life by such practices. Thus, in order to see the true beauty of Islam, we have to remove that debris and uncover the pure Islam while still making adjustments to different climates in which Islam finds itself. Thus I am going to divide our concerns with the prohibited and permissible into different areas and at the end. I will present an actual survey of opinions of different Muslim scholars in the United States on the same questions.

The number one concern is that related to our diet. In Islam, Muslims are told not to eat pork, pork products, alcohol and dead meat. The difficulty is that in may food items, lard is mixed, lard products like gelatin are present, or enzymes from swine or pork are part of the ingredients. Similarly, in many medicines, alcohol is present to a certain degree. My humble suggestion in this area should be that we should make a habit for ourselves and our children to read the labels of all food items and medicines before we ingest them. This is a blessing in this country that we can know what we are eating. In most of the other countries, including Muslim countries, food ingredients are not on the label, therefore we don't know what we are taking in. We should use items which are of vegetable shortening only and do not have a gelatin or enzyme products. Similarly, we should try to avoid any oral medicines which have alcohol in them if we can find a substitute. Many of the cough medicines now are being developed without alcohol. It may happen, although rarely, that a medicine cannot be dissolved in water or other ingredients or especially in injectable forms; therefore, for those essential medicines, we ask God's forgiveness.

In terms of the blessed slaughtered (Islamic slaughter) meat, the controversy in whether God's Name has been invoked or saying, "I begin in the Name of God, the Merciful, the Compassionate" should be done at the time of slaughter or at the time of cooking or at the time of eating the food, preferable, all three. Again, there is no consensus among Muslim scholars if the meat eaten by the people of the book is acceptable to Muslims or not. Many say "yes" using the verse in the chapter al-Maida giving this permission. On the other hand, those who object say that those verses apply to food in general and not for meat because for meat the verse they quoted is from 16:115, which says, "*Do not eat any meat over which name of other than God has been invoked.*" In either case, the blessed slaughtered meat is a healthier meat because the blood and blood products have been drained and the chances of infection and anti-body formation are much less. For the same reason, kosher meats are accept-able to some Muslims although, again, at the time of slaughtering, Jewish rabbi do not use God's Name on each individual animal, but do a prayer in mass. My own suggestion is that one should use only the blessed slaughtered meat if that is available to that person or it is within driving distance. If blessed slaughtered meat is not available and one cannot live without meat, then one has to decide between being a vegetarian versus invoking God's Name at the time of eating the meat. The worse situation will be that those two groups, while insisting on being right, accuse the other group of infidelity or ingratitude and hurt the feelings of the other Muslims and earn the displeasure of God.

The second item is social mixing and dress code for men and women. Both men and women in Islam have a dress code so while women should cover their body's in all areas except face, hands, and feet, men should also be in appropriate dress. The other aspects of dress is that it should not be too tight or too thin, should also apply to both sexes. Muslim women constantly complain that when they put on the head cover, they are iden-tified as Muslim women and thus discriminated against by society. What is the identification for Muslim men who do not have a beard or do not have a cap? Here again are questions of priorities and cultural biases. Some women consider the sari of Indo-Pakistani women an un-Islamic dress because it sometimes reveals portions of the belly. Now on the other hand, the Indo-Pakistani women do not like the skirt showing part of the legs of women as appropriate Islamic dress and consider it as Anglo-French culture. The point I am making is that in Islam, there is nothing like the Arab dress or Pakistani dress. Many Arab Christian women also dress the same way as Arab Muslim women and Pakistani Christian women dress the same way as Pakistani Muslim women. In order to be identified as a Muslim, the women and men should know the guidelines of Islamic dress and try to design their dress according to this. A nice booklet by Dr. Jamal Badawi is available on the title, "The Dress Code in Islam."

In the area of social mixing, the separation of the sexes is emphasized very much in Islam. By this, mixing is meant non-business, intimate mixing. Muslim women in the past and even now in societies where Islam is practiced, have conducted their regular business whether in terms of teaching or nursing by the side of men if both of them have their Islam etiquette in their dress code, manners and talking. Neither of them should dress or behave in a way to incite the other nor should they talk in a romantic way to make some suggestions. Other than that, they can mix while conducting a business or running an organization. Women should be allowed to go to the mosque, to pray and to participate in other important activities in the mosque. However, there should be separate areas for them for such purposes.

Interactions with non-Muslims is another tricky situation. We are asked to spread the message of Islam and give missionary work and take care of our neighbors even if they are non-Muslims, help the poor and needy even if they are non-Muslims, but how do we do these without mixing with them? My solution to this situation is not that we have to stay inside our home or inside our mosques and let those seekers of missionary work visit us. We have to take ourselves and our religion out of the closet and into the open air to expose non-Muslims to practicing Muslims and Islam. The best way we can do this is, first, at the work place, where we do meet non-Muslims and from our words and mostly from our actions and appearance, we let them know we are Muslim and available to answer any questions they may have about Islam and be prepared to answer those questions. Thus it implies that we must learn and practice Islam first before we go out on this venture.

Secondly, we don't have to be forceful in giving such preaching of Islam rather than just give the necessary information and praying to God to accept our effort and give guidance to those who seek it. We have to be pleasant in manner and have wisdom as outlined in the Quran and know the techniques of giving missionary work. However, we must choose our playground. We should not play games on their ground, but should engage in discussions on our terms. We must participate in the interfaith process and visit synagogues and churches, while allowing non-Muslims to visit us during our social functions like the Festival or the post-sunset ending of the prescribed fast so that they may witness the practices of Islam. As far as our children are concerned, we have no choice. Our children will mix with non-Muslims because they do in their schools anyway. We have to set the rules for after-school hours, that is where they should mix. If they must meet and mix with non-Muslim children of the same sex, it has to be in Muslim's house and not in non-Muslim houses where the rules of the game may be entirely different.

SOME HORROR STORIES

Now I am going to describe some of the obsessions with priorities of permissible and prohibited which give the wrong messages. These are real stories and not made up for this article. A Muslim scholar visits my house for a social function. He was not sure I would serve him blessed slaughtered meat so he brings his own food. That surprises everyone else and hurts my feelings. A devout Muslim woman visits the house of another Muslim in a social gathering. Before the food is served, she asks, "Do you serve permissible meat?" The host, obviously hurt, replies, "My faith is very strong, but I do have blessed slaughtered meat for those who have weak faith." The questioner should have used blessed slaughtered rather than permissible or should not have asked any questions at all. The third situation in this area: after my lecture about Islam, a Muslim woman came forward and asked me if McDonald's hamburger is permissible. While answering her, I had to look the other way because her dress was very inappropriate.

Another situation which occurred in a Muslim country. A group of Muslims were arguing whether wearing a platinum ring is permissible for men or not. One group said it was permissible because only gold is mentioned in the Traditions, and the other group said it is not permissible because platinum is costlier than gold and therefore should have the same restrictions. I patiently listened to their discussion while the call to the evening prescribed prayer was being recited from the nearby mosque. I went to offer my prescribed prayer at the mosque. When I come back, none of those people had prayed and they were still arguing about permissible and prohibited. In this regard, a question was asked from me, "Who is better, a Muslim who never performs the prescribed prayer or the one who prays occasionally when in the company of Muslim friends or Muslim boss?" The answer is neither. The former is a disbeliever and the latter is a hypocrite.

Another situation mentioned to me by a young man was that his parents were so strict that they never allowed him to talk to Muslim girls in his mosque or social functions in the community so he did no know any of them. Since he grew up only knowing non-Muslim girls at public school and college, he is going to marry one of them I am not justifying his reasoning or actions.

I was told that in Detroit, a certain Muslim opened a grocery and meat store. He wrongfully included pork in his meat business store. Muslims obviously did not like it and objected to it in a very forceful way. First by complaining to him, then by defaming him to those in the mosque, even to those who evidently did not know him and thirdly by picketing in front of his shop and labeling him a disbeliever. Finally, this person gave up and he had a sign in front of his shop one day when they came to picket. The sign said, "Yes, I am a non-Muslim so please leave me alone." The lesson is that a Muslim is not to push a half-Muslim into disbelief, but try to bring him back by wisdom and beautiful manners if he can do that. Maybe this brother needed more education. Maybe he needed a rich person to buy all his pork meat and throw it in the trash or whatever, but to drive him to declare that he is a non-Muslim was not the best thing that could be done.

Several years ago, I mailed a questionnaire to about twenty prominent Muslims in the U.S. to assess their opinion of lawful and prohibited in social situations while interacting with non-Muslims and the opposite sex. I asked them questions giving real situations from my own experience.

Twelve out of the twenty returned my questionnaire with a response and a comment. They are as follows:[1]

1. In Islam, men and women should not shake hands. However, several of my female patients, especially older ladies for whatever reason, extend their hand to shake hands. What should I do?

Eight of the respondents said that I should go ahead and shake hands as my intentions are pure. Two said that I should never shake hands with women.

Discussion: Even though those who said that it is allowed, they agreed that one should try to avoid shaking hands as much as possible and keep the hands busy otherwise. Two of them who did not approve used the saying of Prophet Muhammad that, "I am a man who does not shake hands with woman," and other sayings, "It is better to be clubbed with a rod of iron in your head than to touch a woman to whom you are not related by Divine Law." The "touch" here is a sexual touch rather than casual shaking of hand. As a male physician, when he takes the hand of his female patient in his hand, he is increasing her confidence and offering a form of psychological treatment. Similarly, Muslim nurses who helped the injured during the battles in the days of the Prophet, had to touch men in order to provide treatment. But those days, taking care of Muslims, not sex, was on the mind of the people. "All of our actions will be judged by our intentions," according to a Tradition of the Prophet.

2. At the annual faculty staff banquet which I had to attend, wine was being served at the table, to which all of them accept except me. What should I do?

Three out of ten said I should leave the table where wine is being served while seven out of ten said I should do nothing and sip my ice tea.

Discussion: Several other comments came to light. One was that maybe the non-drinkers should have a table of their own and if one has to sit at a table where wine is being served, he must explain to others why he is not drinking, giving himself a chance to explain Islam. One of the learned scholars mentioned that in his company, when non-Muslims are drinking, it is their business provided that we do not serve, handle, facilitate, or promote the act of drinking. He said that we should not back out of all such occasions and activities in which non-Muslims are drinking and Muslims have to attend those gatherings because of their status or department position.

3. I am traveling on a plane, tired from lack of sleep, beverages are being served, and my neighbor in the next seat orders a small glass of wine. However, the old lady cannot open the bottle herself and asks me to open it. What should I do?

Seven of the respondents said that I should refuse to open the bottle and three said I should quietly open it and go to sleep.

Discussion: Opening this bottle is equal to serving wine and one should not offer wine to anyone, that one should politely explain to the lady that this is against our religion. Another respondent suggested I should push the call button so that an attendant may come and open this bottle and relieve me from this dilemma.

4. My friends and patients know that I am a Muslim and I do not celebrate Christmas.   But during Christmas-time, they send me many Christmas gifts, candies, and cards, etc. What should I do?

None of the respondents suggested that I should refuse to accept these gifts and all ten suggested that I accept the gifts and thank them and maybe send a nice gift back during '*Id* or other Muslim holiday.

Discussion: The learned scholar who wrote a five-page long response to my questionnaire, mentioned that Prophet Muhammad (ص) accepted gifts from non-Muslims and sent gifts back to Jews and Christians.

However, we must explain to our Muslim friends why we do not celebrate Christmas or the birth of any prophet; we must reciprocate their good will by giving them gifts including gifts of Islamic literature on our occasions.

5. I invited a new non-Muslim faculty member to my house for dinner. He, out of his ignorance about me or Islam, brings a bottle of champagne with him. What should I do?

Six respondents said that I should ask him to take it back while five said that I should take it and destroy it.

Discussion: The learned scholar mentioned that I should take it and destroy it after he leaves, better than in front of the children of my family to remind them we don't drink. We should also explain to our guest why we don't drink It was suggested that returning the bottle to the guest and asking him to destroy it may embarrass him as he meant well.

6. In my office, although I am a Muslim and don't celebrate Christmas, my good secretaries are Christians, and consider this office as their second home, and want to have a Christmas tree or some decorations. What should I do?

Three out of twelve said I should not allow them to have a Christmas tree since it is my office and the boss sets the rule and they should respect my feelings. Eight out of twelve said I should let them practice their religion as my office is their office as well and a Christmas tree is more culture from German tradition than a religious symbol.

I wonder what these eight would say if my secretaries were Hindu and wanted to place and idol of Rama during Diwali.

7. At the hospital, many colleagues, patients, nurses, etc., while walking or in the elevator, will say to me "Have a nice Christmas" or "How was your Christmas?" What should I say?

All said I should give appropriate, short response, i.e., "have a nice day!" and move on.

Comment: Islam is simple and asks us to be polite and humble and even meet bad with goodness and politeness and good nature is missionary work in itself. Goodness of conduct constitutes half of religion.

In conclusion, the guiding Islamic principles in the lawful and the prohibited are:

1. Everything is permissible except that which is specifically prohibited.

2. To make things lawful and to prohibit is the right of God only "*It is not fitting for a believer, man or woman, when a matter has been decided by God and His Messenger, to have any option about their decision: if*

anyone disobeys God and His Apostle, he is indeed on a clearly wrong Path" (33:36).

3. To prohibit the lawful and permit the unlawful is equal to polytheism (associating partners to God).

4. What is permissible is sufficient and what is unlawful is superfluous.

5. Whatever leads to unlawful is also unlawful. Based on this, the mixing of the two sexes and serving or selling wine is prohibited).

6. Good intentions do not make wrong acceptable. For an action to be acceptable, the intentions are to be pure and the action itself must be pure as well. There is no concept of Robin Hood in Islam.

7. Doubtful things (*makruh*) are also to be avoided according to the Tradition of Prophet Muhammad: "The permissible is clear and the prohibited is clear. Between the two, there are doubtful matters which people don't know are permissible or prohibited. One who avoids them to safeguard his religion and his honor is safe while one who engages in a part of them, he may be doing the prohibited."

8. The Law of Prohibition applies to everyone alike, rich or poor, average citizen and the highest official, the illiterate and the scholar. In many Muslim societies, the rich and the powerful get by with all the wrongdoing while the Divine Law is being enforced on the Muslim masses. To the contrary, Prophet Muhammad (ص) said, "if my daughter Fatima is caught stealing, her hand will be cut off as well."

9. The necessity makes the exception (that is, permission to eat pork if no food available to save life).

10. Given a choice, a Muslim should take the lesser of two evils. For example, a Muslim has a choice to buy a house on mortgage in a nice neighborhood versus raising his family in a rented apartment in a dingy neighborhood infested with drug dealers and violence. Which one should he choose?

I will let the reader ponder on this one.

Note:
Those who responded were Dr. T. B. Irving, Dr. M. S. Meghahed (Buffalo), Imam A. M. al-Khattab (Toledo), Dr. Hassan Hathout, Dr. Maher Hathout, Dr. Mahmood Rashdan, Dr. Jamal Badawi, Dr. Muzzamil Siddiqui, Dr. A. S. Hashim, Dr. Moazzam Habib (Indianapolis), Imam Shakir el-Sayyed (Plainfield, ISNA), and one preferred to remain anonymous.

PART II:
EDUCATIONAL CONCERNS

"Recite, in the name of your Lord
who created,
created the human being
out of a (mere) clot of congealed blood.
Recite! Your Lord is Most Bountiful.
He who taught (the use of) the Pen.
taught the human being
that which he knew not" (Quran 96:1-5).

1 ON THE SUBJECT OF KNOWLEDGE AND THE PURSUIT OF EDUCATION

The first order of God to mankind was *"iqra"* or recite. This command is given to Prophet Muhammad in the cave on Mt. Hira as the first revelation. This command was intended for all of humanity and not only for Prophet Muhammad (ﷺ). *"Recite in the Name of your Lord who created the human being out of a mere clot. Recite and your Lord is most bountiful. He who taught by the pen taught the human being which he knew not"* (96:1-5)..

These verses emphasize three points: First of all, the source of all knowledge is God Almighty. Secondly, He taught us the use of the pen (therefore, the importance of writing); and thirdly, we were created by a mere clot and we did not know.

The first point is elaborated in another verse, *"It is He who brought you forth from the wombs of your mother. You did not know a thing, and He gave you hearing, sight, and mind in order that you may give thanks"* (16:78). The second point is elaborated in a Tradition by the Prophet who said, "The ink of the scholar is more sacred than the blood of the martyr." The third point is restated in another verse of the Quran, *"We have not given you the knowledge except a little"* (17:85). The Quran again reasserts, *"Are those who have knowledge and those who have no knowledge equal? Only the men of understanding are mindful)"* (39:9).

On this point, once the Prophet (ﷺ) was asked to compare the learned (*alim*) to the worshipper (*abid*). And he said the learned has superiority over the devotee in as much as I have over the average Muslim."

SAYINGS OF THE PROPHET

In addition to above sayings, the Prophet (ﷺ) has been known to say the following (see Bukhari):

1. To seek knowledge is a duty for every Muslim male and female.
2. Seek knowledge from the cradle to the grave.
3. Seek knowledge even if you have to go to China.
4. To listen to the words of the learned and to instill into others the lesson of science is better than religious exercises.
5. Acquire knowledge. It enables the possessor to distinguish right from wrong. It lightens up the path to the heavens. It is our friend in desert, our company in solitude, companion when friendless. It guides us to happiness. It sustains us in misery. It is an ornament among friends, and an armor against enemies.

I am confident that words of God and His Messenger are enough to make us understand the value of enhancing an education. However, one western educationalist has correctly said, "Only the educated are free. The rest of us are slaves of those who have monopoly on knowledge."

Muslims of those days were not like Muslims of today who, after listening to the Word of God and His Messenger, returned to their homes and went back to their daily routines. Those Muslims took orders literally and were determined to acquire knowledge. They obtained knowledge from the Persian, Roman, Indian, and Greek cultures and assimilated into Islamic knowledge. They developed science, technology, and medicine. They fought wars only to get a few rare books. They awarded the translators with gold. They contributed to medicine, philosophy, algebra, alchemy, and astronomy. They were the torch-bearers in the Dark Ages. It was only when they lost this determination that their decline started.

"KNOWLEDGE IS NOT ENOUGH"

Knowledge has no meaning unless it be translated into action. The Quran has correctly attached belief to the right action together in many ways. The Quran says, *"It is a grievous matter in the sight of God that you say that you do not do"* (61:3). And again, *"Will you enjoin what is right on others and forget yourself"* (2:41).

So it is obvious that acquiring knowledge or preaching it to others is not enough. The Prophet (ص) said, "Humanity will perish (in the hereafter) except the learned. The learned will perish except those who act upon their knowledge. Those who act upon their knowledge will perish except those who are sincere, and even in the case of those who are sincere it is precarious." Thus our actions are a testimony to our own belief in the knowledge we have.

Let us give you some examples from day-to-day life. If one has passed the written exam for driving, but he doesn't apply it on the road test, will he get the license, and if he doesn't apply it in daily driving, is he not sure to have an accident? If a soldier learns how to use a machine gun, but never fires one, the difference between him and the instruction manual is the difference between a living and dead source of knowledge. To a physician, one gentleman comes with symptoms of bronchitis and is given a prescription for antibiotics. He takes the prescription, keeps it safe on the highest shelf, reads it five times a day, even memorizes it, even kisses it out of respect, but never goes to the drug store to get the drug and use it. Is it possible that he will ever get well?

The Quran is the prescription for our well-being and our illness, physical, mental, social and financial. On the Day of Judgment, we will not be tested of our knowledge. There will be no multiple choice quiz on our Islamic knowledge. We will be asked what we did with our knowledge. Iblis (Satan) was a very knowledgeable *jinn*. In fact, he was appointed to teach angels, but we know what happened to him when he did not apply his knowledge of God's Omnipotence and refused to bow as ordered.

Finally, I want to say a few words about childrens' education. Some parents are more concerned about their children's Islamic education than their own. I feel children live in the shadow of their parents. We should be what we want our children to be, then they will be what we want them to be. We can't make your child Muslim by having him memorize a few words or verses from the Quran, or telling them how to perform the prescribed prayer. We have to perform the prescribed prayer with them, perform the prescribed fast with them, show them a good Muslim and keep them in the company of Muslim children.

2 SECULARIZATION OF HIGHER EDUCATION: AN ISLAMIC PERSPECTIVE

It is refreshing to note that Islam is being included in this seminar. In the past, such seminars have taken place in this country for many years without inclusion of Islam or Muslims. This attests to the fact that the Judeo-Christian society is slowly moving toward becoming a Judeo-Christian-Islamic and others society. The concept of "melting pot" is changing to "salad bowl" in which all of the ingredients are encouraged to display their distinct flavor and taste rather than melt down into one flavor. In this country, there are approximately 6 million Muslims and about 50,000 Muslim students enrolled institutions of higher learning though the exact figure is not known. There are close to 120 chapters of Muslim student associations (MSA) tied to the national organization. Islam is being taught, usually by a non-Muslim faculty, either as a separate course or a part of Middle Eastern studies in many universities. Muslim students are organizing seminars and functions directed toward bringing them together and opening dialogues with non-Muslim friends and faculties.

Secularization evolved in response to a dogmatic religion which rejected scientific theories as blasphemy. I agree with the previous speakers that in the institutions of higher learning, the secularization is directed toward trivialization of religious devotion. Religion is given a tertiary place, the primary being science and secondary being social pleasures. The down-sizing of religion is due to elimination of God from daily life.

Some folks would like to confine the God to a house of worship be it a mosque, a synagogue, a temple or a church where they can visit Him when they feel like it one day a week but would not allow Him to leave those places and enter their homes and influence their lives. Thus religion becomes a personal matter second to more important things in life although religion came before the government, before the politics, the science and television. Students realize that studying religion may not give them the financial satisfaction for the material life they aspire for. Thus only whose who are left out from going into better paying professions like Engineering, Science, Medicine, Accounting, Law, etc. end up in places of religious learning such as seminarys and Traditional centers of learning. Many young people and their young faculty during college years take a vacation from religion because they see religion regulating their life style. The new freedom included freedom from God, because without God, everything becomes possible in their vain desires and behavior.

The religion of Islam is not a way of worship to a God. It is a way of life. The emphasis on education in Islam is described well in First Revelation which says: *"Read in the name of thy Lord who created man from a clot and read thy Lord is the most bounteous who taught you by the pen, taught man that he did not know"* (96:1-5).

A question is asked in Quran, "Are those equal who have knowledge and those who do not have knowledge?" The knowledge in Islam is basically of two types: a) the knowledge of God and b) the knowledge of His rules. By the former, we must learn Who created us and for what purpose and how do we conduct our affairs and to whom we return. We know God through his attributes described in the Quran. By the latter, we mean all the knowledge which now is called, "secular or scientific knowledge," such as physics, chemistry and biology is all knowledge of God's rules. Once we discover "something,," we call it a scientific discovery although that entity was there to begin with. We have just learned it now. One of the purposes of education is to liberate ourselves from ignorance and prejudice which leads to mistrust of one another. In this regard, only the education of each other will bring us together in respecting each other's beliefs and honoring each other's life and property. The prevailing misconceptions about a religion are not reflective of the original teachings of the religion. Thus it is important that comparative religion be taught to each student in a basic form from a purist source.

What should be done to combat the secularization of higher education? The following are my suggestions.

1. Teaching of Islam in universities and colleges should be done more seriously and not superficially. At the present time, the courses are not sufficient. At a freshman or a junior level, one hardly gets an exposure to the religion of Islam and his or her knowledge of the religion is usually derived from the way it is projected in the media. The teaching of Islam should include the history, the life of prophet Muhammad, the shariah or Islamic law, the philosophy, the moral, the political and economic system of Islam.

2. If Muslims are not qualified to teach Judaism and Christianity, why should others be teaching Islam? By this, I mean every attempt should be made to have a Muslim faculty teaching Islam to non-Muslims.

3. I also recommend that Muslim Student Association chapters be established in each college and university which have enrollment of three or more Muslim students. One of their functions should be to engage non-Muslim students and faculty in a dialogue in order to understand each other in a better way. Appropriate behavior of each religion group should be well-defined. Thus I am proposing an Interfaith organization in each institution of higher learning be developed.

4. Stereotyping of Muslims and ridiculing their religion because of whatever happens in the Middle East should end. Mutual tolerance should be encouraged.

The seeds of centuries-old hatred and mistrust between religions in the old country should not be allowed to be sown into the fertile soil of the new land. We Americans should not only be leaders of the world in science and technology, but also in the interfaith understanding through preservation of religion in the higher education. We must not repeat the failed experiment of Communist countries nor should we contribute to further ethnic cleansing.

The purpose of learning Islam by non-Muslims in American universities should also change from helping American missionary, soldiers, businessmen, and foreign service officials understand the religion of Muslims when they go to Muslim countries to understanding the religion of six million fellow citizens who are here to stay in order to bring them into cooperation rather than confrontation.

3 BLUEPRINTS FOR EFFICIENCY AND EXCELLENCE FOR MUSLIMS

Islam is a dynamic religion. It spread like wildfire from Arabia in every direction and changed the shape of the world and the mores of people. It put order in their lives and made each faculty subservient to God. Thus they acquired and utilized knowledge and invented machines and medicine. For six hundred years, Islamic culture and science were the dominant factors in much of the civilized world. Knowing Arabic was a must for all scholars, Muslim and non-Muslim alike. Three hundred years before Pasteur's discoveries, Muslim scientists pioneered algebra, chemistry, and medicine. Muslims made the first calculators and the astrolabe. In Europe, which was in the Dark Ages, Muslim Spain was flourishing. Cordova had a population of 500,000 compared to the 38,000 in Paris. It had 700 mosques and 900 public baths. It had sidewalks and street lights while most of Europe was dark. In every field they were the best people during those days. And they are attributed to bringing Europe out of the Dark Ages due to the interaction and exchanges taking place during the Crusades. Most voyagers like Christopher Columbus used Muslim navigators to help find new lands. God Almighty has fulfilled His promise in the Quran: "*You are the best community that has been raised among mankind. You enjoin what is right and forbid indecency and you believe in God*" (3:110).

71

But what has happened to us now? Individually, while working for IBM, a Muslim may be the most efficient employee, but collectively, our efficiency and excellence has gone down. We hardly work except for a few. Look at the bathroom in a mosque and in a church or a Holiday Inn. Compare the streets of Karachi to those of Paris. We come late to the office, to parties, to appointments, unless it is with a non-Muslim boss. We don't take good care of our health. We are nowhere to be found in modern discoveries and scientific advancements. Everybody makes fun of us as dagger swinging terrorists, riding camels and keeping harems, none of which are true. Even our enemies joke about us: Moshe Dayan, the Israeli Defense Minister once said, "Do you think the Arabs can ever beat you?" He replied, "Not until they first learn how to make a straight line while boarding a bus." After the U.S. F-16 crashed over the Gulf of Sidra during the Libyan Crisis, the Pentagon official said, "They (the Libyans) can't even shoot a banana in the air." The present day lack of efficiency and excellence in Muslims in general is due to:

1. Lack of knowledge and skill.
2. Lack of self-esteem and dignity.
3. Laziness and lack of hard work.

Success is tied to belief and practice. Let us examine them individually.

LACK OF KNOWLEDGE AND SKILL

Much has been said about this issue to this point. To recite" or to read,"*iqra*" was the first order of God Almighty to mankind. But Muslims hardly read these days except for a few. It is much easier to watch television, movies, and gossip rather than read a newspaper, a serious book, or a scientific article. Writing is an even harder job. Have they not read: *"Are those equal, those who know, and those who don't know?"* (39:9).*"The blind and the seeing are not alike, nor are the depths of darkness and the (genial) heat of the sun"* (35:19). Prophet Muhammad (ص) placed much emphasis on acquiring knowledge and skills.

LACK OF SELF-ESTEEM

After 200 years of colonial rule, we Muslims not only have been robbed of all our treasures like the Kuh-i Nur diamond, but also of our dignity and we have accepted the "superiority" of the Anglo-Saxon race.

We are told that we are barbarians, terrorists, illiterate, and fanatics.

Everything related to us, be it our color, our accent, our culture and even our sand is of inferior quality. We have accepted the cultural slavery of our former colonial masters. Sometimes we even feel guilty about being Muslims as we fail to identify ourselves as Muslim in our outlook or behavior. We have forgotten that man was created in the best mold and should not become the lowest of the low (Surah at-Tin). The difference between the best of creation and the worst of creation is faith in God (Surah al-Bayyinah).

LACK OF HARD WORK AND LAZINESS

We Muslims in general have acquired the reputation of being late and lazy. It is shown in the performance of office workers, factory workers, and students. In the house the man hardly moves to get a glass of water, much less to speak about helping his wife. It seems that we have no motivation to excel. We are even lazy in our duty to God and many of us miss the dawn prescribed prayer. *"Whoever strives hard, he in fact strives for himself"* (29:6).

We have forgotten the dignity of labor. Our Prophet used to work with his own hands, be it cutting meat, sewing or gathering wood. All prophets were shepherds A companion came to the Prophet, and the latter wanted to shake his hand. The companion hid his hand behind his back, saying, "O Prophet, my hands are dirty. I am just coming back from work, and I don't want your hands to become dirty," The Prophet took his hand and kissed it, saying, "Hellfire will not touch the hand of a worker." We also don't have value of time. We waste time in gossip, backbiting, watching useless programs on TV, listening to unhealthy music, and sleeping more than necessary. Time is the precious gift of God. We don't even have time to spend with our family, to take care of ourselves with exercise or to advance our knowledge. Time is like melting ice, and if we don't use it, it will be gone. Remember, whatever we want in the next world we must accomplish in this world. Thus by wasting time, we are in fact, damaging our future.

The clues to success are tied to self purification and belief: *"Successful is the one who purifies himself"* (97:14). *"He who purifies himself, in fact purifies his soul"* (35:18).

Features of believers (*al-mu'min*) have been described in the Quran at many places. Let us review and find out how many we have in us. In

Surah al-Mu'minun, the believers are described as those who are humble in their prayer, avoid vain talk, pay *zakat*, and guard their modesty. In Surah at-Tawba, they are described as those who protect each other, enjoin what is right and forbid what is wrong, and strive in the cause of God. In Surah al-Infal, they are mentioned as those who when God's Name is mentioned, feel fear in their hearts. When the Quran is recited it increases their faith. They trust their Lord. They establish worship and spend from what God has given them. In Surah ar-Rad, they are described as those who keep their trust, have patience, avoid suspicion and spying and do as they say. Thus as mentioned in Ale-Imran, verse 110, God's bestowing on us as being the best community which has been raised for mankind is based on three conditions: First, we enjoin what is right conduct (and practice it ourselves too); second, we forbid indecency (and avoid it ourselves, too); and third, we believe in God (and show it with our actions). Finally, if we want to get back our lost glory we must do it ourselves. *"God does not change the condition of a people until they change what is in themselves"* (13:11).

4 GUIDELINES FOR ISLAMIC STUDY CIRCLES

The following guidelines consist of an introduction, a description of the nature of Islamic Study Circles, a suggested organizational structure, a format and approach to the study of the Quran and Traditions, rules of the meeting, physical arrangements, a children's program, suggested list of topics and time table example and, finally, a list of suggested books and resource materials.

By the grace of God Almighty, Islamic awareness and desire to know more about Islam is increasing. In every town, small or big, one or more groups are being organized to learn the Quran and the Traditions. We hope,with the Will of God, He will accept our efforts and reward us by bringing change in our way of life to total submission to his Will.

The purpose of this article is to present a formal outline as guidelines to organize and sustain such efforts. Based on fifteen years of experience, I also offer what problems to except and offer some practical solutions.

NATURE OF ISLAMIC STUDY CIRCLES

Islamic Study Circles are not a substitute for the Sunday school or weekly adult meetings on Sundays. ISC meetings are for those who are seriously committed to change their lives in accordance with the teachings of Islam. Each participant should prepare for the meeting and contribute in the discussion. It should be limited to a maximum of eight families. Although they should be encouraged to continue their weekend Islamic activities, the concept of "weekend Islam" should be discouraged.

ORGANIZATIONAL STRUCTURE

It is observed that many problems in such circles are due to lack of effective leadership. Therefore, as recommended by Prophet Muhammad (ﷺ), whenever there are three or more people we should elect an Amir. The Amir should have qualities of piety (*taqwa*), leadership and organization. Amirs should be better than others in recitation and knowledge of the Quran. They should be fair to everyone and humble in nature. They should be able to delegate some of their duties to their assistant. They may appoint group leaders among children to promote leadership. The duties of the Amir should include scheduling the meeting, informing in advance, assigning the topics and format, and presiding the meeting itself. Communication is the key to the problem and solution. Most problems arise out of mis-communication. I personally believe newsletters are better than phone calls due to uniformity of message.

FORMAT

There is usually controversy regarding the format, i.e. whether to start with topics, or the Traditions (*ahadith*) or the Quran first and which part of the Quran, i.e. from the beginning to end or otherwise:

STUDY OF THE QURAN

We should not rush through the Quran since it is the comprehensive book of wisdom and knowledge. It is reported that Abdullah Bin Umar took eight years to finish the second chapter, Surah al-Baqarah. He used to read a verse, memorize it, practice upon it and then proceed further. Even if we read at a fast pace of one section (*ruku*) a week it should take us several years to finish the Quran in ISC gatherings. Emphasis should be made on individual efforts daily at home and assimilating and incorporating the message of the Quran. First, we should gather authentic commentaries, i.e, Yusuf Ali, Pickthall, Asad, Maududi, Mufti Shafi, Ashraf Thanvi Ibn Kathir, Sayyid Qutb. We should also obtain recitation tapes, i.e. from Shaykh Minshawi, Basit and Hussary.

The format should be like this, i.e., if the discussion is on the first chapter (Surah al-Fatihah), first the tape of recitation should be played so that everyone can listen and correct their pronunciation. The Amir should listen to the recitation of members and correct them, if necessary. Then one English and one Arabic, Urdu or other native language translation be given. Then the Amir or chairperson who has prepared should give a brief summary of the commentary, not from his or her imagination but from one of the authentic commentaries. This should be followed by a general discussion or comments. An attempt should be also made by individual members to memorize some or all of the verses under discussion in the same setting or at an hour before the session.

STUDY OF TRADITIONS

At least one Tradition (*hadith*) could be discussed from the authentic books, i.e. Bukhari, Muslim or collection of forty Traditions or the Sacred Traditions (Hadith Qudsi, in which God spoke in the first person to the Messenger, but they are not included in the Quran). The Traditions (*ahadith*) should be read in Arabic and English and the resource person should be able to explain the context in which the Tradition was cited and how it applies to our present life.

STUDY OF TOPICS AND LITERATURE

According to the wishes and deficiencies of the members, topics may be selected by the group and assigned in advance to be presented in a concise manner quoting again not the imagination, but the Quran, Traditions or authentic books of commentary, i.e, *Halal Wal Haram* by Yusuf Qardawi or many pamphlet by Maulana Maududi. The speaker may want to listen to Jamal Badawi's tape on that topic beforehand and make a summary of that presentation. The topic may alternate with the presentation of various Traditions.

CONDUCTING THE MEETINGS OF THE ISC

The meeting should start with the recitation from the Holy Quran followed by other items on the agenda (see example) and should end with a prayer or supplication. General Islamic code of manner of conducting meetings should be observed.

    a. One person to speak at a time with the permission of the Amir

    b. No whispering or talking to others while the Quran is being recited or explained.

    c. Speak in low voice.

    d. Do not interrupt the speaker but let him or her finish first.

    e. The Amir should be fair to everyone and allow them to express themselves with restriction that such discussion be 1) after the presentation 2) related to the subject 3) not based on personal opinion but preferable from the Quran, Traditions, or noted authority.

f. The Amir, or the speaker should again try to avoid his or her own opinion but give answers from the Quran, Traditions or say one of the schools of jurisprudence.

g. Avoid talking about a person if he or she is not present in the meeting, even if what is being said is true.

PHYSICAL ARRANGEMENTS

It is advised that the meeting be held on a carpeted floor in form of a circle, than around a table. Men should be in a separate area of the same room. Everyone should be modestly dressed. There should not be any mixing or joking between the men and women. Questions should be directed to the Amir and not to individual people.

RULES OF THE MEETINGS

a. Frequency: Meetings can be held once a month, twice a month, or once a week, depending on the level of interest and time available.

b. Timing: It should be according to what is best for the members. I believe Friday evening between evening and night prescribed prayer is the best, leaving the weekend for other social activities and Sunday school.

c. Place: Can be in one central place or by rotation at the house of members. Again good communication is needed to avoid misunderstanding.

d. Punctuality: This is the key to the success. If anyone is planning to be late or absent, they should call the Amir in advance, so that others are not left in waiting The Amir should be able to come up with a good excuse in the next meeting. It is our experience that people make a point of attending a function if they attach importance to it.

CHILDREN'S PROGRAM AT ISC

Though participation by children in each program is very important for the purpose of bringing them together, it does not replace Islamic efforts at the Sunday school or individual efforts by parents themselves at home.

The children's program should be short and sweet, no more than 15 minutes total and should include topics on the life of the Prophet (ص), listening to newly memorized Surah, Traditions, presentations, and Islamic knowledge.

Based on their efforts, small prizes can be given once a month to encourage participation and completion.

SUGGESTED TOPICS

A) Quran: Start with 1) 30th part
                or 2) al-Baqarah
                or 3) al-Nisa
                   4) al-Maida
                   5) al-Hujurat

B) Topics: Prescribed prayer (*salat*), the poor-due (*zakat*), the hajj, prescribed fasting,, jihad, usury (*ribah*), the modest dress, permissible and non-permissible food, family life or social problems.

C) Life of the Prophet as:
                   - Husband
                   - Father
                   - Teacher
                   - Soldier
                   - Leader
                   - Negotiator
                   - Missionary

SUGGESTED TIME TABLE
(THIS WILL CHANGE WITH THE SEASON)

PM

5:45	- Gathering time
6:00	- Evening prescribed prayer
6:15	- Start the program with recitation of the Quran
6:30	- Children's program
6:45	- Quran Commentary and Translation
7: 15	- Traditions, jurisprudence or topic
7:30	- Prayer or supplication and Adjourn
7:35	- Snack, tea and social hour

8:00   - Night prescribed prayer
8:30   - Disperse

SUGGESTED BOOKS AND RESOURCE MATERIALS

1. Quranic translations:	Yusuf Ali Translation
	M. Pickthall Translation
	M. Maududi Translation
2. Traditions	40 Ahadith (Al-Nawawi) Qudsi
3. Lawful and Prohibited	- Yusuf Qardawi
4. Way to the Quran	Khurrum Murad
5. Islamic Manners	Madni Abbassi
6. Islamic Teaching Tapes	S by Dr. Jamal Badawi

ADDITIONAL SUGGESTED BOOKS FOR MUSLIM HOME LIBRARY*

1. Seyyed Hossein Nasr, *A Young Muslim Guide to the Modern World*. Chicago: KAZI Publications, 1994.
2. Seyyed Hossein Nasr, **Muhammad: Man of God**. Chicago: KAZI Publications, 1994.
3. Maurice Bucaille. *The Bible, Quran and Science*. Paris: L'Oeille, 1986.
4. H. Abdalati. *Islam in Focus*. Indianapolis: ATP, 1986.
5. Suzanne Haneef. *What Everyone Should Know About Islam and Muslims*. Chicago: KAZI Publications, 1986.
6. R. M. Speight. *God is One*. New York: Paulist Press, 1992.
7. A. Maududi. *Towards Understanding Islam*. Leicester: Islamic Foundation, 1986.
8. Martin Lings. *Muhammad: His Life from the Earliest Sources*. Vermont: Inner Traditions, 1990.
9. Laleh Bakhtiar. *Muhammad's Companions: Essays on Some Who Bore Witness to His Life*. Chicago: KAZI Publications, 1993.
10. Murteza Muttahari. *Islamic Modest Dress (hijab)*. Chicago: KAZI Publications, 1991.

* All titles and materials above are available from KAZI Publications, Chicago.

PART III:
POLITICAL CONCERNS

"And why should you not fight in the cause of God
and of those who, being weak,
are ill-treated (and oppressed)?
Men, women, and children whose cry is:
'Our Lord! rescue me from this town,
whose people are oppressors;
and raise for us from You
one who will help!'" (Quran 4:75).

1 THE CRISIS IN THE MUSLIM WORLD AND THE RESPONSE OF AMERICAN MUSLIMS

Prophet Muhammad (ص) had said, "The nations will gather against you like those who are invited to a feast while they are starving." The companions asked, "Is this going to occur when we will be few in number?" The messenger of God (ص) replied "No, you will be in large numbers, but you will be like the foam, that floats on the ocean. Your enemies will no longer fear you. The *wahm* will be in your heart." They asked what is *wahm?* He replied, "The love of this life and fear of death."

Let me first explain the magnitude of the problem. While it is true that Muslims are one billion in number, I believe there are too many zeros in that billion. While it is true that there are 52 independent countries, they are subservient to those who gave them independence. While it is true that Muslims control half of the world's oil fields and 40 percent of natural resources, that money is being used for the West. While it is true that some of the richest people on earth are Muslims, yet most of the Muslims live in poverty and below the standard of human dignity. There are 20 million refugees in the world who are homeless, driven out from their own land, and 80-percent of them are Muslims. Since 1979, from the invasion of the Red Army to Afghanistan until now in 1993, I have figured that at least 5 million Muslims have given their lives in all of the wars and catastrophes which have been imposed on them. That includes close to 1.5 million in Afghanistan and close to 1 million in the Iran-Iraq war, a war which was imposed on Iran by Saddam Hussein, then the friend of the West, close to one-half million in the Iraq and U.S. war, or what is called, "Operation Desert Storm" and another large portion in the present who are in former Yugoslavia. Of these 52 Muslim countries, they have a total of 4 million superbly trained armies but these governments and their armies are busy fighting Islam in their own country; therefore, they have no real power to fight the enemies of Islam.

Let us examine the weapons and tactics of our enemies. After nearly 200 years of colonization and ransacking of Muslim countries and stealing their diamonds and natural resources and subjugating them to all kinds of oppression, they have been given so-called independence. However, with the independence comes the revival of Islam and also the liberation for Muslims in the former colonial powers. Thus, in order to defame Islam and Muslims, we have been labeled terrorists, hostage takers, hijackers and backward people. If you look at the world, it appears that Muslims are victims of the state-controlled terrorism as you see in Israel and former Yugoslavia rather than those who are terrorists themselves. The problem of terrorism is not of the religions but rather a struggle between those who have not and those who are oppressed and those who are oppressors. Thus you will see that there is a lot of violence in many countries where there is no Muslim presence. Looking at their own history, it was not Muslims who started or maintained the Second World War. These people who love blood killed nearly 20 million people in the Second World War and another 4 million people in the Vietnam War and you see in Korea, South Africa, South America and in Ireland, there is a lot of violence and bloodshed where there is no Muslim involvement.

While they have accused Muslims of spreading Islam by the sword, the sword never reached in most of the countries which have 90-percent Muslim population like Indonesia or many parts of Africa. They themselves have used the latest weapons to annihilate or destroy Muslim populations including the use of chemical bombs, cluster-bombs, Tomahawk missiles, all kinds of weapons as they have been used in Operation Desert Storm. While they accuse Muslims of making Islamic bombs, they themselves are the ones who have used two atom bombs to destroy two cities in Japan and killed close to a million people.

They have used and are using food as a weapon as one sees in Somalia, Iraq, Eriteria and in Sudan where close to four million people have died in the last several years. They have used water as a weapon as one sees the water problem in Jordan and Israel Muslims are not known to run any concentration camps and cause genocide but they have done it to themselves in the Second World War and now they are doing this is former Yugoslavia. Now, according to the reports by Amnesty International and Physicians for Human Rights, the mass rapes which are happening in Bosnia and in India are not just a male instinct or occasional incident by certain army soldiers. They are using this for what they call, "ethnic cleansing." This should be better described as "ethnic pollution" since those people are very proud of their heritage and of their purity. In order to destroy their honor and heritage, it became necessary for them to pollute them by raping their women and impregnating them. In Bosnia alone, close to 50,000 women have been raped out of which 35,000 became pregnant. After raping these women many, many times, they were not allowed to leave these concentration camps until they became pregnant and pregnancy reached the later state that abortion could not take place. This has all been published from a report published recently in *Newsweek* and also reported by Physicians for Human Rights which sent a team to investigate the war crimes. In their desire to subjugate and humiliate Muslims forever, the forces of the West and of Israel and the Jews and Hindus have combined under the umbrella of the United Nations. God says in Quran,, "*When it is told to them, 'Do not make mischief on the earth,' they say, 'We are peace makers only.' They are indeed the mischief makers, but they perceive it not*" (2:12). Thus under the pretext of making peace, UN forces are indirectly or directly sometimes supporting the oppressors in Bosnia and elsewhere.

Now let us see what the real reason is behind what is happening in all these places of trouble. The reason there are Muslims in Bosnia and surrounding states is not because of forceful conversion by the Ottoman army. In fact, the Ottoman army was invited to make peace between the warring factions of the Roman Empire and Eastern Orthodox in the 13th to the 14th century. Subsequently, many of the Ottoman army soldiers settled down and it is through their conduct and invitation that many of the local residents accepted Islam. There are close to 4 million Muslims in that area; however, now they are being driven out from their own land and close to 200,000 have been killed and 400,000 have been injured in the war in Bosnia. The Muslims of Albania and other neighboring states are under direct threat from Serbian forces. What is happening there is the worst fear of having a Muslim state in Bosnia. One of the Serb leaders in Kosovo has said that we are fighting this war to save Europe from Islam.

In a research document presented to the House Committee on Foreign Affairs, it was pointed out that these researchers thought that at least 65-percent of Muslims in Europe are involved in Islamic activities and thus are a threat to the West. After Serbia has occupied 70 percent of Bosnia. To enforce the Vance/Owen peace plan on Bosnia is to accept the status quo of the land which has been grabbed by Serbs and in fact, dividing with them what they got illegally and also not questioning their war crimes and their murder, rape, and concentration camps, etc.

Now let us change our direction to Somalia. What happened in Somalia, which was colonized by British and Italians after the Second World War, is the direct result of the cold war between the United States and the Soviet Union. They both dumped weapons and encouraged sections to fight each other. A well-known dictator, Said barre, was installed just like Marcos in the Philippines who ruled with an iron first for twenty years under the protection of the United States and when the Soviet empire fell, there were a lot of weapons left in the country and that is how the infighting started between the tribal forces and secular forces as well as Islamic forces. Close to 1 1/2 million people have already died of starvation and another two million are starving. So this peacekeeping and humanitarian effort was started but as published in a newspaper recently, the real reason behind such humanitarian effort was something different and these were: 1) oil has been found in Somalia and it will become a state like Kuwait in terms of its oil capacity and production and 2) there is a strong tendency in Sudan for making an Islamic state and in order to contain that Islamic government in Sudan and also to punish Libya who are the neighbors of Somalia, a force has to be there to do so. So from the strategic location of Somalia, the forces which will be there will be able to control not only Sudan, Egypt, Ethiopia, and Libya, but Oman and Saudi Arabia will also be able to direct and control the flow of oils and weapons to and from Iran. The acting U.N. Secretary General has been urging the United States to disarm the Islamic forces in Somalia and also later on in Sudan where just recently the Pope visited and gave his ultimatum.

Now let us turn to India where close to 120 million people are Muslim. Such a large number, which is twice the population of France and nearly half the population of the United States, cannot and should not be considered a minority. However, the majority is five times more. Thus, the Hindus had developed a plan for their own ethnic cleansing.

They accused Muslims of being the invaders although the Aryans themselves were the invaders in India. Thus the recent drives in which the historic Babri mosque was destroyed by militant Hindus and there were close to an additional 20 or more mosques elsewhere which have been destroyed in India. Close to 10,000 Muslims have been killed and thousands of Muslim women have been raped. India's secular status and non-violence is totally exposed to everyone. Historically, Hindus have blamed Pakistan for all of their problems but the Babri mosque was not destroyed by Pakistani agents nor in Bombay were the Muslims killed by Pakistani police.

To get rid of such a large population of Muslims in India, it would be difficult but not totally impossible. The Muslims are being given a choice —either you become Hindu or you die or you leave the country. Some Muslims are bowing to these pressures. They have begun to be assimilated in the melting pot. Inter-religious marriages are becoming common in India and there are many secular and Communist Muslims. Urdu became a victim or oppression and thus a lot of Islamic history and culture and values were lost by the new generation of Indian Muslims by losing Urdu. India's desire to occupy and brutalize the people of Kashmir, where the Muslims constitute the majority, has been present for the last 5 decades. All the human rights organizations in the world have confirmed the atrocities of burning houses and killing people and raping women in Kashmir because the people of Kashmir wanted their own state. The West's double policy of granting and supporting independent democratic states in eastern Europe and in Russia does not apply when it comes to Kashmir. Thus the weak and innocent people of Kashmir are suffering and continue to bleed until the help from God comes.

What about Iraq? Iraq as the former seat of the Caliphate was always a sore eye in the eyes of the West and a crusade could not have been completed without destroying Baghdad. Thus, first the Iraq-Iran war was started in which close to $5 billion of Muslim money was used to make them fight each other and kill close to a million people and then Iraq would not be kept alive as a threat to Israel or other countries; therefore, it has to be destroyed itself. Thus with the help of Muslim rulers and Muslim money, close to $632 billion, the destruction of Iraq was accomplished Again Amnesty International and Physicians for Human Rights have extensively described the damage done to civilians in this war. Close to 200,000 soldiers died but more than that were the civilians in the city, especially the children who were the target and 90-percent fell on hospitals, homes and bridges and then to complete the suffocation, total economic blockage took place to bring down the Iraqi people to their knees. At this moment, Iraq has unofficially been divided into 3 portions. The southern portion, where there is a no-fly zone, is totally controlled by the U.S. which still has a presence of 20,000 troops and 100 combat aircraft and another portion which is kept as a buffer zone between Turkey and central Iraq. This zone was created to help so-called Kurdish people but is actually to subjugate them from Turkey. They have frozen all of Iraq's assets which are close to $50 billion just like they froze $30 billion of Iran's assets in the western bank as a means to reduce the $1 trillion deficit.

What about Israel? It was created as an illegitimate child in the heart of a Muslim country in order to serve as a police state and an extension of the West's arms policy. It is being given close to $5 billion a year in military aid so that it will develop weapons and test on Muslim land and flesh. Human rights violations in Israel are of no concern to the West. Israel deported 450 Muslim Palestinians to a no-man's land. These people were born in Israel and they are university professors, doctors, and other intellectuals in no way linked to the PLO or any other terrorist organizations. In the Intifada, close to 5,000 young boys and girls and children died by so-called rubber bullets of Israelis for the crime of throwing stones. The Palestinians who have been living in tents for the last 40 years are living under subhuman conditions with no education, very little water, very little food and torture. Their human rights are not considered to speak of. In 1992, reports by Amnesty International have outlined very well the human rights violations by Israel in Palestine.

What about the southern Russian Muslim Republics? After the break-up of the Soviet Union, six Muslim republics were created of which Tajikistan is in the worst shape right now as Communists are fighting the democratic movement soon after the creation of the republics. The U.S. Secretary of State, Mr. Baker, was sent to tell them they should never support any Islamic movement in those countries nor should they try to be friends with neighboring countries like Pakistan, Afghanistan, Iran, and Turkey. Thus, the Communists in Tajikistan were encouraged to kill their own people. 100,000 of them have now migrated to Afghanistan and many died on the way. The Russian Army along with Uzbek forces have been doing the same there which the Serbs are doing in former

Yugoslavia. The only difference is that in Western papers, you don't hear much about these things because the sufferers are Muslims.

What about Burma? Muslims have lived since the 17th century in large areas of Burma joining what is now Bangladesh and have enjoyed a rich culture and governed themselves for 350 years. However, now the Buddhists who are the majority in Burma were encouraged to call the Muslims invaders and they are now being persecuted and being killed and being deported to neighboring Bangladesh. Again, these Muslims, like the Muslims of the former Yugoslavia, or Kashmir, are not being persecuted there because they are terrorists or members of the PLO but they want to identify themselves as Muslims and lead a life of Muslim as ordained to them.

So they are being persecuted and we hardly hear much in the Western reports because there is no oil in that section of Burma just like Bosnia is Kuwait without oil fields. In Indonesia, Muslims are in the majority. The real rulers are secular Western dictators like Suhardo or his Christian associate, General Madni. Thus, with the encouragement of the United States and Church leaders including the Pope who has visited there, while Islam is being suppressed, Christianity is being encouraged to flourish. It is a real threat that in a few years, the population of Java will be changed to become a Muslim minority.

Now I want to turn your attention to that state of Islamic movements in Muslim countries. We cannot blame the Hindus, Christians and Jews for all of the sufferings of Muslims. We have to assume some responsibility ourselves too. Islamic movements in Muslim countries are being persecuted under the direction of the secular governments installed by the former colonial powers. Thus, in Turkey, we see that the government is doing its best to fight the Islamic revival and prosecuting Muslims in large numbers. It has also, for years, been oppressing the people of the Kurdish area. No wonder that since Turkey is engaging fighting Islam, it cannot use its forces to fight for Islam. Wearing the modest dress is banned for Muslim women in Turkey if they are attending universities. In Algeria, 82-percent of the people voted in October 1991 to elect an Islamic government. In Saudi Arabia, many many Muslims, and especially Islamic scholars and ulama, are being persecuted and put in jail for opposing the introduction of foreign troops on that soil in the Operation Desert Storm. In Syria, the secular government has been fighting Islamic brotherhood and has now come to some kind of compromise to share power with them. In Egypt, Nasser, Sadat, and Mubarak all were and have been engaged for the last 40 years in crushing the Islamic revival and movement while encouraging leftist and secular Muslims. Special torture cells and prisons were created in which Muslim brotherhood members were tortured for many years some of them I know personally. By encouraging Coptic Christians, Egypt is on the verge of breaking into a northern Christian and a southern Muslim state. Similarly, both in Morocco and Tunisia, it is dangerous to be identified as a practicing Muslim. Islamic movements are banned while the Jews and secular Muslims are in power.

Under these circumstances, what should be the role of American Muslims? We are a number close to 6 million in this country. We have the most educated Muslims of the world gathered here and it is true that we can practice Islam better in this land of freedom than many Muslims can do in their own country. Thus we have an obligation to establish Islam here.

First of all, this crisis in the Muslim world has renewed a new awakening among us to be aware of the sufferings of Muslims all over. We have to learn to recognize our enemy, the enemy outside our ranks and enemies within our ranks. We have to learn that God's help will not come unless we fix ourselves first. Our first agenda should be to establish Islam in our own self and in our family and in our community where we live.

Establishing Islam to me does not necessarily mean memorizing verses of the Quran or just performing the daily prescribed prayers, but it is a comprehensive idea to include the tools of survival which are our physical well-being, a spiritual and moral well-being, economic strength, educational pursuit, and political expression. We cannot live in a shell or in a closet or preach Islam from the top of a *mimbar* nor should we come down to the foot of the hill in order to melt in the melting pot. We have to identify ourselves as Americans while Muslims by the way of life.

We have to share the sufferings and the concerns of all Americans irrespective of their color or religious background. We have to be part of the mainstream political process to become a voter and express ourselves. We should be able to educate fellow Americans about the sufferings of Muslims in Muslim countries and Muslim minorities in non-Muslim countries and be able to explain why they are being oppressed. We also need to express our solidarity with Muslims in Muslim countries in a justifiable cause. This support we can give in our speeches and writings by monetary and other means. We should join in hands with human rights organizations in this country and form also an independent American-Muslim human rights organization to monitor the human rights violations in Muslim countries. We should coordinate our efforts to have a better impact rather than a hundred different organizations doing the same thing.

Finally, we should send a message to the oppressors that the Muslims of this country will not tolerate what is happening the Muslims in Bosnia, Kashmir, Somalia, and all Muslim countries that we cannot conduct business with oppressors, be Hindu, Jew, or Serb, in a normal relationship unless they stop oppressing our people. Most importantly, we should trust in God as He has directed to us in the Quran. God says, "*If God is your helper, no one can overcome you and if He withdraws His help from you, who is there to help you, in God do find believers put their trust*" (3:160).

Brothers and sisters, be aware that we are not the chosen people. If we do not do our job right, then God will choose someone else to do this job. He says in the Quran, "*God is free of all wants and it is you that are needy. If you turn back from the path, He will substitute in your stead another people, then there would not be likes of you (timid and weak-hearted)*" (47:38). None of these things we can do either in this country or elsewhere unless we have unity among them ourselves and the only criteria for such unity is that we are believers who are conscious of God. Thus to remind us again, God says"*All of you believe, observe your duty to God with right observance and die not except in a state of submission to Him and hold fast all of you together the rope of God and do not get disunited and remember, God's favor on you how you were enemies and He made friendship and love in your heart so that you became brothers by His grace and how you were on the brink of fire and He did save you from it. Thus God makes clear His revelation to you that you may be guided and let there be from you rise a nation which invited people to goodness and enjoins right conduct and forbids indecency. Such are those who are successful*" (3:102-104).

2 REFLECTIONS ON THE GULF WAR

"*O children of Israel, remember the special favors which I bestowed upon you and that I preferred you over other nations (for My messages)*" (2:122).

I thank Rabbi Sasso and my friends at Beth El-Zedeck Hebrew congregation for inviting me to express my thoughts about the Gulf war. Let me start by clarifying my position. First. I am a physician, not an American politician who remained quiet when Saddam invaded another neighbor ten years ago and used chemical weapons on its own people but race against each other to ridicule and defame him when the media tells him to do it now. I am not here to defend Saddam. As a member of Physicians for Human Rights and Amnesty International, I was aware of his torture of political prisoners, use of chemical weapons and the treatment of POW's between 1980-1989 and I tried to draw attention of Muslims in my writings and Friday's sermon but at that time Saddam was portrayed as a friend of the West, a great Arab leader, and a moderate (a term used by Bob Dole). In my remarks against certain U.S. policies, I am not trying to be anti-American. I am just with hundreds of thousands of Americans, one of them burnt himself to death, who are opposed to war and are for peace. I am a U.S. citizen, I donated my blood to save the life of my American non-Muslim patient. I am dedicated to the interfaith dialogue and I provide voluntary free medical care to the poor and homeless. Please do not label me an anti-American.

I am also not here to defend Islam, apologizing for Saddam. Islam as a way of life, in submission to the will of God, is above those who can defame it by their actions. Islam cannot be judged by the behavior of some terrorists and secular leaders, just as Christianity should not be judged by the behavior of crusaders, Nazis, IRA, Red Army, and individuals like Rev. Jim Jones, Charles Manson, Harvey Oswald or David Koresh.

In the last 1,400 years, Islam has survived many attempts to wipe it out, i.e., crusades, destruction of Baghdad by the Tartars, the fall of Muslim rule in Spain and in India, liquidation of Ottoman Empire, invasion of Afghanistan, Iran-Iraq war, and God willing, it will survive this war too.

SOME FACTS AND FICTIONS

Yes, I opposed the invasion of Kuwait by Iraq and support the need to liberate it. However, there is strong evidence that Iraq was lured into invading Kuwait, the green light being given two days before by our own Ambassador in Baghdad. Critics call it a joint conspiracy, in the pretext of liberation of Kuwait to destroy and occupy Muslim lands. Thus the 100,000 army sent to defend the House of Saud, swelled to a 700,000 army invasion with 3,000 war planes and more than 100 warships from Australia to Portugal and Argentina.

No such force and urgency was shown by those who pretended they opposed aggression when Soviets invaded Afghanistan and killed 1 million Afghans, disabled 2 million and displaced 4 million of a country of 10 million. I wished Afghanistan had oil and a corrupt Amir with savings in U.S. banks. If Iraq destroyed 10 percent of Kuwait after the invasion, the rest of the 90-percent was done by the allied bombing. If Iraq killed 10,000 Kuwaitis (a hypothetical figure), allied bombings would have killed 200,000 Iraqis by now and will kill nearly a million by the time the war ends. Remember the figures for the Vietnam War were three million and World War II was 20 million and those wars were not started by terrorists or fanatic Muslims.

The West feared Saddam's nuclear capabilities and has bombed them twice but the real threat to the world is from the civilized West who have used the atom bomb to destroy two cities in the past and are always willing to do again. The chemical weapons possessed by Iraq were the ones given to Iraq by West Germany and the U.S. companies In 1920, the British were the first ones to use poison gas shells in fighting Iraq's revolution. The U.S.A. opposes taking "hostages" and using them as shields but did not "intern" 100,000 American Japanese in the concentration camps during World War II. What is the difference in the words?

The war was inevitable as everyone wanted it. The U.S. defense contractors and oil companies wanted to make more money. The Pentagon wanted to test new weapons on Muslim lands and flesh. Arab kings and shaykhs wanted someone else to defend their harems. The neo-crusaders wanted to come back to Baghdad. The Israelis wanted to get some Arabs killed, destroy Iraq's war capabilities, grab half of Jordan to settle more Soviet Jews and extract 13 billion dollars to rebuild a few houses damaged by SCUDS. Even those Muslims who opposed the war saw it as the only means to make the Allied Occupation Army leave their land.

What have we achieved? Saddam wanted the oil to sell at $22/barrel, the war has levelled it at $20/barrel. He wanted Kuwait and Saudi Arabia to write off a 30-billion dollar loan they gave him to wage the war against another neighbor. By refusing, they had to hire "white slaves" as Arthur Schlessinger put it in the Wall Street Journal. So far it has cost nearly 100 billion dollars and it is growing at a rate of one-billion a day now. What will be left at the end? The blood will have dried. The corpses will be burnt, in a "parking lot" called Iraq and a war torn land called Kuwait, to reinstate the corrupt Amir and his 52 wives.

THE NEW WORLD ORDER

It is Saddam Hussain who in fact wanted to start a new world order. He failed. The previous established world order was that only the super-powers or their surrogate client states could do terrorism, i.e., the invasion of Granada, Panama, Afghanistan, Goa (near India), Lebanon (near Syria and Israel), attack on Iran by Iraq, etc. However, with the help of the tonic supplied by the scientist, the monster grew so powerful and said,, "I can do terrorist acts now without the help and support from my Masters." That's where he went wrong and the previous world order had to be rediscovered as "the new world order."

Who is going to suffer most by Saddam's action and the Allied response to it? The most human losses will be by Muslims, especially Arabs. Of course, the economy of many other Muslim countries who depended on such foreign workers have been destroyed. Historically, we Muslims have given our blood to change the course of history. The latest example was that of Afghanistan where one million innocent Muslims gave their lives to stop the Soviets from reaching warm waters. It was the human and financial losses suffered at the hands of Mujahideen that weakened the Soviet grip on Eastern Europe and broke the back of Communism. The domino effect from the fall of Afghanistan is seen in the crumbling of the Berlin Wall. Thus no one should rejoice at the flowing of Muslim blood. It may in turn and in due course crumble their own Berlin wall. God is Just and cannot allow injustice to prevail for long. *"Wrong not and you will not be wronged,"* says the Quran.

Sometimes I wonder why Muslims are being persecuted now. We are not the one who accused the Jews of killing Jesus, or of causing the plague in Europe. We did not kill 15,000 of them in France in 1380 nor 6 million of them in the Holocaust. In fact, we welcomed and let them flourish in Muslim Spain when they were being persecuted in all of Europe. They suffered with us with the Spanish inquisition and they were not allowed to pray in public just as Muslims were not allowed. They followed us to Morocco and to Egypt where Maimonides became the personal physician to Saladin. Saladin sent Maimonides to treat King Richard of England. King Richard wanted Maimonides to stay in England, but he returned to his Muslim boss, where a temple was erected and stands now in honor of this great physician and philosopher.

If this can happen in the past, it can happen again. We can live in peace, if we accept each other as fellow human beings and feel the pain and agony of others. For how long will Palestinians continue to live in tents and refugee camps devoid of basic necessities including clean water, sanitation, and schools which remain closed? For how long will innocent Israeli children and old men have to wear gas masks? The answer to these two questions is tied together and it is peace, not the peace which reigns in the graveyards of Normandy and Hiroshima, but the peace that we should have within, with ourselves, our family, our neighbor, our community, the nations and the world around us.

Finally, how are we American Muslims taking this war? We are told in the Quran, *"Seek help with patience and prayers, for Allah is with those who patiently persevere."* The FBI is watching us for terrorist acts.The public and the media are suspicious of us. Our loyalty and citizenship are being questioned We are supposed to be the one doing terrorism, but we are the victims of terrorism in the U.S Our mosques have received bomb threats. Our children at school and women at the malls have been taunted upon. Employers have suspended some Arab employees. But we have faith in the U.S. democracy and the Bill of Rights. Be assured that we will neither be interned nor deported. We are here to stay.

At the end, I want to refer again to the Quran." *We ordained for the children of Israel that if any one killed a human being unless it is for murder, or mischief on Earth, it shall be as if he had killed the whole mankind, and if he saved a life, it would be as if he saved the whole mankind."* (5:32).

I was in Houston on an interfaith panel on Medical Ethics and I quoted the above verse of Quran about the sanctity of human life. Rabbi Segal said, "This is also mentioned in Torah." I said, because both the Torah and the Quran have the same author."

3 MIXING RELIGION AND POLITICS IN ISLAM

I have been asked to comment on the subject of mixing religion and politics in Islam and how my religion helps me make political decisions. Before I go any further on this subject, I must define our concept of religion and God. To some, religion may be a way of worship or doing some rituals for the God. For us, our religion is a way of life which teaches us not only how to worship Him, but how to deal with others and how to conduct ourselves during our journey on this planet. In Islam, there is no separation of Church and State as I will explain later The concept of God is not only that of the Creator, but also the Law Giver and Sustainer. We do believe that after creating the human being, He left the human being on earth to decide for himself or herself what he or she wanted or how he or she should govern himself or herself. But the human being was created with a definite purpose as stated in various verses of the Quran. In the beginning, we learn when God says, "*I will create Adam as vicegerent on earth*." A vicegerent is like a deputy administrator or assistant principal who does not make his own rules, but continues the rules and laws of his boss. In fact, the human being was placed on earth to establish the rule of God. In the second place, we learn when God says, "*I have created human beings and jinn only to worship Me*."

Now the word "worship" is a comprehensive word that not only includes the ritual of worship, but also obeying God in every possible way, submitting to His will as much as possible. In the third place, God says, "I have created life and death so that I can test which one of you is best in conduct." Now if there is a life hereafter and if there is a heaven and hell, there has to be a criteria of who will go where. Thus we believe that we are being tested throughout our life how we conduct ourselves. In Islam, the real ruler of the State, then, whether called king or president, is God himself. The elected official we call the president or the prime minister, is only second in command since he himself has to follow the rule of God. Thus the elected official is not only accountable to the public or the people who elected him, but to his creator to whom he has to return to give an account of his deeds. The broader sense of this caretaker governor in Islam is that the whole community is responsible and not an individual. The community of believers has been instructed, *"Let there arise a nation among which will enjoin what is good and forbid what is evil."* Thus, the servants of God and His laws can not remain neutral to wrongdoing or injustice.

The second area I want to clarify is the role of the prophets. Prophets were needed from time to time to bring God's message to humanity. The prophecies were basically of two types—good news for those who are believers and righteous that they will be rewarded for their good deeds in the hereafter and as a warning for those who were disbelievers in God and His books and were rebellious towards Him from time to time for the consequences of their actions in the hereafter. The Prophets role was not to make people believers, but to give the message. A prophet is also not to make his own laws, but either to explain the laws of God or deliver it as such like a postal carrier.

The third category is that of a ruler. The ruler or the caliph is again a vicegerent to the Prophet. Now he does not inherit prophethood from the prophet, but only the message the prophet was carrying, The ruler or the caliph implements that to his best capacity. The Quran says, *"The believers are told to follow God, the Prophet and the ruler above them."* In this injunction, it is implied that the ruler has to follow God and the prophet. If the ruler does not follow God and the prophet, the people are not obliged to follow the ruler. In fact, if he is oppressing people, which is against Islam, the people have an obligation to stand up to this ruler even if he is a Muslim. This is from the saying of Prophet Muhammad (ﷺ) to stand up to a tyrant and speak a word of truth as one of the best forms of *jihad*. The ruler in Islam, whether it is the prophet or subsequent caliphs, is not only the administrative authority, but is also the highest religious authority.

Thus, church and state become one in this situation. Even in the past, many religious leaders like the Popes who called for the crusades and Archbishop Marcos or Khomeini continued to exert political influence through their religious authority. Even now it is said that Pope John Paul's visits to many countries like Sudan, Indonesia, and South America have a political message for their regime. He also influenced the fall of communism in Poland by supporting the Solidarity movement.

Now after this introduction, I come to the topic "How My Religion Helps Me Partake in the Political Process." I must vote for the candidate who is righteous and whose ideology is close to my own religious ideology. He must be against homosexuality, drugs, and abortion. He must support a welfare state, taking care of the poor, needy, homeless, the minorities, and support spending on education and health care. He must be able to fight violence and crime. He must have popular support and come through the democratic process. The democratic process in Islam is called "*shura*" or consultation. This means that the leader has to be elected by mutual consultation and he must have pledge of allegiance from those who elect him. He also should be helped with a consultative council to make decisions rather than make all of the decisions himself. A candidate should have a sound, moral character in his own personal life in terms of his family life as well as him financial accounts. If he cannot be trusted by his family in his character or by financial institution in financial matters, then he should not be trusted by me either to make decisions for the country.

Thus, my response on domestic political issues is derived from my religious convictions. The head of the state which is elected in Islam is a leader of believers and not necessarily a leader of convicts and rapists. Therefore, criminals do not have the same rights as non-criminals and, thus, the ruler's obligation toward a good citizen is different from that of wrongdoers.

In the international field, my political decision is not based on my allegiance to a piece of land either outside or inside this country. We do not consider a global interest as my own interest. Thus we must support the human rights movement in any part of the world whether it is Muslim or non-Muslim. We must oppose oppression in any form whether the oppressed are Muslim or non-Muslim. The height of patriotism is to oppose the ruler whose actions are not in the best interests of the land or the people. If we say that we believe in God and trust in God as our coin says, we must make Him the ruler in all of our affairs. We do have an emotional, an ideological sympathy towards what is happening to Muslims in Bosnia, Kashmir, Palestine, and Somalia. However, we have no sympathy toward any Muslim leader in any of the Muslim countries who is not following Islam and applying it for himself or his fellow countrymen.

Does my religion call for blowing up of World Trade Center and airplanes? The answer is definitely "No." Islam believes in the sanctity of human life and therefore we have no affiliation with those who do wrong and happen to have a Muslim nam. Peace in Islam, is not the absence of war, nor through war We do not encourage the peace which prevails the graveyards of Normandy and Hiroshima. By peace we mean, peace and justice, peace with honor and peace through submission to Will of God. By peace, we mean to be at peace within our own self, our family and community, our neighbors, peace at both the individual and collective level, above all to be at peace with our Creator.

Islamic response to oppression is described in the Quran is the following way, "*And why should ye not fight in the cause of God and of those who, being weak, are ill-treated (and oppressed)? Men, women, and children whose cry is: "Our Lord! rescue us from this town, whose people are oppressors; and raise for us from Thee one who will protect; and raise for us from Thee one who will help!*" (4:75).

The wrong means do not justify the right cause and there is no concept of Robin Hood in Islam. Does my religion call for the execution of an oppressor ruler? The answer is "No." If the ruler is not a practicing Muslim, in fact, doing un-Islamic things, he should be removed by a democratic process and not by a coup and bloodshed.

If Muhammad (ص) wanted to establish Islam by the wrong methods, he would have made a terrorist squad of people to kill the leaders and unbelievers in Makkah and establish himself as king. He did not do that. He spread the message and once the people became Muslim, they created an Islamic state in Madinah We must be bold enough to tell the oppressor that he is doing wrong and never bow down to his wrongdoing. We don't have to become violent to do that. We might be persecuted for opposing him. We might be exiled for doing so, but in the long process, if we conduct ourselves in a civilized way, we may be able to replace him with a better ruler. In Islam, mixing politics with religion is not only permissible,but it is possible because politics are subservient to religion itself.

However, doing wrong things as some politicians do these days, would not be Islamic. In this way, the wrong and the right cannot mix together. Religious leaders and political leaders, instead of opposing each other, can help each other by advising each other, both submitting to the same God they worship together, for the benefit and welfare of ordinary citizens.

CONCLUDING REMARKS

50% of eligible American voters who do not vote allow the 50% of those who do to elect officials who will influence our lives through policies and decisions they make on the local, national and international levels, in terms of employment, education, pollution, prices, defense, morality, war and peace, etc., etc. Sometimes evil flourishes when a few good people do nothing to oppose it. The religious communities should realize that participation in the political process is not only their right, but their duty. If unopposed, the secular forces in pursuit of life, liberty, and happiness will prevail to establish the ever changing and sometimes conflicting rule of human beings. On the other hand, we, the religious community, are also for the pursuit of life, liberty, and happiness, but as defined by our Creator. What is good for us is also good for humanity. In this regard, all religions are on the same side of the fence. Instead of opposing each other, they should join hands in their common fight against crime, homlessness, immorality, injustice and racism. American Muslims, the newest factor, should not only concern themselves with self preservation, preoccupation or with international conflicts, but join their other like-minded Americans in their fight against abortion, homosexuality, pornography, teenage pregnancy, discrimination against women in minorities, better education, housing and employment for all. United we stand and divided we fall. American Muslims must come out of hibernation and let others see them, have their voices heard and opinions known. They must register as voters and join one party or remain independent. They should communicate with their congressmen, senator, mayor, governor, and other elected officials. They should write letters to editors on all issues and not just in reaction when Islam is attacked. They must actively participate in improving community relations and political advocacy.

4 REFLECTIONS ON BOSNIA
AND THE HOLOCAUST

Today we have gathered to commemorate the fiftieth anniversary of the Warsaw Ghetto Uprising and see how it relates to the people of Bosnia On April 19, 1943, 50 years ago, the Nazis moved onto the Warsaw ghettos with plans to liquidate the 60,000 Jews remaining there after 400,000 had already died from starvation. With almost no support from the outside world and few arms, 1,300 Jews resisted this Nazi action and held off fully-armed German troops for 27 days. Now history has repeated itself after 50 years again. Not far away in Europe, 60,000 Muslims are packed into the town of Srebrenica refugee camp which, after a long resistance of several months, has now surrendered to the Serbian Army who are also doing "ethnic cleansing." This thing happened again in history because "evil flourishes when good people do nothing to oppose it."

I am glad to be in the company of so many young Americans today. We have great hope in their peace movement. It was the peace movement by young Americans in the sixties which finally helped to stop the bloodshed in Vietnam. I am happy also to be in the company of artists, musicians, and poets. They are very sensitive people. They understand the sufferings of humanity and in their talented way, can express this is their art.

The previous speaker, Jeanette Hablallah, spoke about what is happening in Bosnia in terms of the killings, torture and rape, but at the beginning of her speech, she told how different she looked being a

Muslim woman compared with the rest of the crowd. As a physician who has spent two years in anatomy, I must tell the youth that this difference is superficial only. Once you remove the skin, the flesh is the same color, the blood is the same color, and the bones and the nerves are the same color. So the difference between you and me and among yourselves is not how we look, but how we behave. There are some who are peace-lovers and human in their behavior as the people who have gathered today to hear about what is happening in Bosnia. Also, there are some who may look like you, but they are animals in their behavior in killing innocent people, raping women, and torturing many many people of all ages and sex. They are Serbians.

This event is sponsored by the Peace and Justice Center to which I am very thankful. I want to ask a question, "Is there any difference between peace and justice and justice and peace or are they the same?"

The first category describes that we must have peace by any means and then justice will prevail. We Muslims do not believe in the peace that reigns over the graveyards of Normandy, Hiroshima, nor of concentration camps, or of holocausts because a lack of peace is due to injustice. In order for peace to be established, justice must prevail first. We have an example of this in the second verdict in Los Angeles. If people had accepted the injustice after the first verdict and there was no opposition to it, there would have been non second trial and, therefore, justice would not have been established to insure peace as it happened after the second trial.

The Serbians say they are a superior race and want to get rid of others including Catholics, Croatians, Muslims and Bosnians and establish themselves as a great Serbia. For this, they are doing what is considered "ethnic cleansing." Close to 400,000 people have died. Close to two million have been made refugees in Croatia Close to one million people are disabled, and close to 65,000 women have been raped. Out of that, according to Physicians for Human Rights reports, 35,000 became pregnant. They were not allowed to leave these "rape camps" until the pregnancies reached to the extent that abortions could not be performed. This was the Serbian way of insuring a Serbian child in that land.

The humanitarian and medical needs of those unfortunate people are great. I am a diabetic specialist and I was told by the Diabetes Association that there are 75,000 diabetic patients who are without insulin. Many of them are dead by now, most likely.

Let's discuss what we can do. Fourteen-hundred years ago, a great man said this, "If you see a wrongdoing, try to stop that by your hand; i.e. do everything possible in your power to stop that wrongdoing." Most of us are not in a position to do that He said, "If you are weak and cannot stop the wrongdoing by your hand, then try to stop it with your tongue;" i.e., you should speak against it, you should write against it, and you should educate people and start a movement so that somehow those that have the power of the hand will realize this wrongdoing. He said that, "If you are so weak that you cannot stop it with your tongue, then at least feel bad in your heart and that is the weakest of faiths." That was Prophet Muhammad (ص).

My dear friends, being neutral to a scene of injustice is equal to contributing to the continuation of injustice. Therefore, we cannot remain passive spectators to what is happening in that part of the world, or, as a matter of fact, anywhere in the world where people are being oppressed. What is happening there can happen here 50 years from now. We must do whatever we can in the weakest position that we may be by donating our money, by donating our time, by calling our congressmen and senators, by calling the President, writing letters to the editor, and organizing a movement; whatever we can do, we should do it. None of you are too weak to do anything. When you go home tonight, after having a good time of music, food and drink, think of all those women who have been raped and having pain, think of all of those women who have lost their brothers and husbands, think of all of those men who have lost their wives and daughters, and think of those old men who have lost their children, their homes and everything. How can we sleep with happiness when there is so much suffering for our fellow human beings?

My dear friends, let me tell you, if there is a God, He is testing us to see how we respond to these human sufferings. If we are not able to do our job, His patience may run out and He may take matters in His own hands. And if He does that, He may not only punish the criminals, the Serbians, but also their silent partners, like us. I hope that does not happen. So as we gather today to commemorate the holocaust and the Warsaw ghetto uprising, we must tell the world, "No more holocaust, no more Bosnia, enough is enough."

Peace by upon you.

5 VIOLATIONS OF HUMAN RIGHTS BY THE WEST AND THEIR CLIENTS IN MUSLIM COUNTRIES

This paper is dedicated to Prophet Muhammad (ص) who was sent as a "mercy to mankind," who was always on the side of the weak and the oppressed, to all those people who have been persecuted and given their lives for His cause, to all those who are still being oppressed and to all those who are doing something about it, be they Muslims or non-Muslim, may God help them (*amin*).

There has been considerable interest developed in the last decade in the monitoring of human rights in the Third World. Countries are being rewarded or penalized according to their compliance. However, it appears that everyone is looking at someone else's record and not his own.

In this paper, the history and western concept of human rights is outlined, followed by the description of the violations both by the superpower and the Muslim countries, especially in relation to the torture of political prisoners. Finally, the basis of Islamic human rights, the Quran is used to warn the oppressors of their wrongdoing and to activate the masses and the intellectuals to oppose this injustice against innocent fellow humans.

God Almighty says in the Quran: "*Do not cause mischief on earth after it has been set in order, but call on Him with fear and desire (for His mercy), Lo the mercy of Allah is always near to those who do good*"

(7:56). However, mischief makers consider themselves peacemakers: *"When it is told to them, make not mischief on earth, they say we are peace makers only. Behold! They are indeed the mischief makers, but they perceive not"* (2:11-12).

Their second problem is that they also consider themselves to be champion of human rights. In January of 1989 in Vienna, Austria, the U.S., Western European Nations, and Warsaw Pact Nations met and agreed on a human rights accord to "enhance" freedom in the Soviet Bloc countries. They also held an international conference of some 31 nations in 1991, in Moscow! Yes, after killing nearly one million Afghans, injuring another two million, displacing some five million from their homes with the most sophisticated weaponry in the world, now the Soviets are hosting a human rights conference.

Let us examine the records of these so-called champions of human rights. They claim that the world got the concept of human rights in the 12th century from the British document called the Magna Carta. But between the 12th and 17th century there was no mention of the practice of human rights by them (i.e. trial by jury or the rights of taxpayers). Only in the 18th century in documents such as the Constitution of France or the Declaration of Independence in the U.S. do we see the mention of the rights of people. Even in later documents, the words, "We the People," mean only white males. Abigail Adams, wife of John Adams, who was one of the authors of the Constitution, wanted women also to have voting rights. But American women did not win their voting rights until 1920— more than 800 years after the Magna Carta was written. Blacks, as slaves were denied all rights,al though 5000 of them fought against the British for the independence of America. They did not receive their full civil rights until the 1960's.

These proponents of human rights, the inheritors of the Magna Carta, did not apply it to others. They killed American Indians by the thousands, and enslaved the remaining few in reservations. They got hold of Africans by hunting them in the fields of Africa, bringing them chained on crowded ships, where 1/3 died during the journey. They denied them their religion, stripped the of their names and honor, and put them on plantations as slaves. When the first British fleet arrived in Australia in the 18th century, it forgot to take the Magna Carta with it, and systematically destroyed the Aborigines. In 1788 the population of the Aborigines was

300,000, and in 1901 they numbered only 93,000. Even now they are being persecuted. Their unemployment rate is 30%, compared to 7% for the whites. Their life expectancy is 18 years less than the whites. The Aborigines got voting rights only in 1967. Even in prison they are being killed and tortured. Since 1980, more than 103 Aborigines died in prison (20 times the rate of the whites).

On December 10, 1948, the United Nations adopted the Universal Declaration of Human Rights. Since then, are these champions of human rights complying to do something about it, if it concerns blacks, Muslims, or other Asians or South Americans? Since 1984 in South Africa, hundreds and thousands have been killed, including 312 children. According to Amnesty International, political prisoners in South Africa were tortured with electric wire, strangulation, beating and burning. Amnesty itself has compromised its credibility and integrity by consistently maintaining a mysterious silence about the treatment of Palestinian prisoners in Israeli jails. Palestinians in Israel prisons are subjected to horrifyingly inhuman treatment of both physical and mental torture intended to cause permanent physical and mental impairment. According to a report in the Wall Street Journal, the only toilet facility provided to Palestinians in Israeli prisons is a bucket and many Palestinians released from Israeli prisons have lost their physical and mental dexterity due to the torture inflicted upon them in Israeli prisons. Since the recent Palestinian uprising (Intifada), nearly one thousand youths have been killed, at a rate of five a day. Palestinians are being deported from their homeland, their houses burned or razed. Small children are fighting the mechanized Israeli army with pebbles and stones. And those rubber bullets are really of lead covered with rubber and are nearly as dangerous as the real lead ones. One may wonder why these human rights activists do not speak up loudly to undo injustice; I'll tell you why:

When they talk about human rights, they talk about their own rights, the rights of the western European races and of Jews, but not of Third World people, including Muslims, Blacks, South Africans, Red Indians, or South Americans. Everyone is pressuring the Soviets to grant asylum to the Jews there, but no one is talking about the plight or the rights of 30 million Muslims in the Soviet Union and five million Muslims in the Soviet-controlled by Eastern Europe. Even the Americans have not given full rights to all of their people; their women are still fighting for equal pay, job discrimination, sexual harassment, while nearly four million are severely beaten up every year. The same happens to Hispanics, who just won a lawsuit against the FBI for discrimination in employment and promotion. What about the Second World War? While the U.S. was fighting both Japan and Germany, it put 120,000 Americans of Japanese origin (but born in the U.S.) into concentration camps in deserts as prisoners of war, where thousands died. Only in 1988 did Congress agree to compensate them for their loss of property. However, the enemy of their own color, i.e., the Germans born in the U.S., received no such treatment as the Japanese-Americans did. American injustice is not always limited to race, color, or religion. From 1900 to 1987, 350 alleged criminals were hanged by U.S. courts, only to have their innocence proven later. The dual standards of American are well known; while the U.S. never compensated Iran for the loss of 290 civilians in the 1987 shooting down of a civilian Iranian airbus, it has demanded 30 million dollars from Iraq for the loss of 29 marines when the USS Stark was attacked by the Iraqi Air Force by 'mistake'.

FREEDOM OF SPEECH

We should take with a "ton of salt" the Western misconception about the absolute freedom of speech, which according to some is a relatively new idea and amounts to the imposition of the western value system upon the Third World. By giving this right to Salman Rushdie, they gave him, and themselves, the right to slander, defame, and ridicule others. They themselves have a dual level of tolerance. Thus, when many world leaders, including religious leaders like Cardinal O'Conner of New York and Rabbi Jakobovitz of England and many others, expressed their views against the *Satanic Verses,* those views were not published in the U.S. media. When former rock singer Cat Stevens (Yusuf Islam) endorsed the death sentence on Salman Rushdie, his songs were boycotted by radio stations and his records were broken in public. This dual standard is not new. While secretly and now officially the U.S. continued to deal with the PLO, but when Andrew Young, the only Black American ever to represent the U.S. at the U.N. shook hands with a PLO delegation, he lost his job. His other crime was saying, "There are still thousands of political prisons in U.S. jails", meaning Blacks who had been arrested and prosecuted in U.S. jails without a proven criminal charge."

The American artist who displayed the U.S. flag on the floor and made people walk all over it said in a press conference, "I did so because the U.S. flag is a symbol of oppression to millions of people around the world." He and his family received death threats. When some wanted to burn the sacred U.S. flag as a test of this inborn and absolute freedom of expression in the Bill of Rights, there was nationwide turmoil from newspapers to the Presidency, and flag burners were not only labeled anti-American, but arrest and prison sentence was called for them. Thus, these people who define freedom of speech and writing, and give it only to themselves or their illegitimate surrogates like Salman Rushdie to defame and slander others with an "inferior" value system. They never give the same rights of free speech to others. For example, Prime Minister Margaret Thatcher's government pressured many parts of the "white commonwealth" to ban Peter Wright's book *Spycatcher* in which she was criticized. When Professor Ali Mazrui mentioned in an interview on BBC/PBS television program that Karl Marx was the last of the Jewish prophets, it was censored in the U.S. and not aired. No western defender of the freedom of speech came to defend his rights or the rights of Yusuf Islam.

HUMAN RIGHTS IN ISLAM

Some 600 years before the Magna Carta, Islam gave the concept of total human rights. Islam recognized the fetus as a human being and gave it the rights of inheritance after birth. Islam recognized human beings as dignified individuals who have the right to equality, personal freedom, liberty, personal opinion, emigration, justice, and social welfare. Even the poor due (*zakat*) is not a charity, but the right of the poor over the wealth of the rich. In family matters, there is the right of the husband over the wife, and vise versa, that of the parent over the children and vice versa. The rights of the neighbors were so much stressed that Prophet Muhammad (ص), at one point, thought God might ask us to include our neighbors in our inheritance.

There are many books written about human rights in Islam. I advise the reader to seek these rights directly in the Quran or in a book based directly on the Quran and *sunnah*. One of them which I highly recommend is *Al-Islam wa huquq al-insan* by Dr. Mohammed Khoder and translated into English by Dr. Zaid A. Al-Hussain. The basic difference between Islamic human rights and Western human rights are these

a) Islamic human rights are universal and apply to all men, women, and children irrespective of their race and color. In practicality, man-made human rights serve the interests of the people who made them and their people.

b) Human rights given by God are inflexible, while human rights made by humans change according to the ambitions of their administrators. Thus, Teddy Roosevelt, after conquering the Philippines, said, "The only reason we are here is to Christianize the people."

c) While the western concept of human rights concerns mainly certain sections, i.e., the rights of Jews to migrate, Islamic human rights encompasses all sections and apply to all nations.

VIOLATION OF HUMAN RIGHTS IN MUSLIM COUNTRIES

After saying that Islam gave us human rights before the Magna Carta and UN resolution, and that we have a better product, let us examine what is being practiced in Muslim countries inside their prisons.

The records of the USSR, and countries of the West and even Israel should not provide us with a reason to condone or ignore the dismal records of many Muslim countries and the violation of human rights of their own Muslim population which is tantamount to the sinful disregard of the teachings of Islam. The Soviet Union and the countries of the West have at least succeeded in protecting the human rights of their own majority in their respective countries while violating the rights of the minorities or the rights of those living outside their boundaries The sad and undeniable fact is that in many Muslim countries, human rights of the Muslim majority are violated by the leadership in power, and even Muslim religious scholars and intellectuals seem to express little concern.

My interest in the condition of political prisoners in Muslim countries started in 1978 when I examined an Egyptian scholar, in exile in the U.S. for chest pains. I noticed marks of burns and injury on this chest and back and enquired of their origin. At that point, he told me he had spent 14 years of his life inside Nasser's prison for being a member of Muslim Brotherhood and an associate of Shaykh Hassan Al Banna. He described how he was kept hungry and thirsty for days. He was made to stand in a 2' by 2' cell with four others for weeks, without sleep. He was tortured in many ways and even made to drink his own urine. His story was confirmed by another associate of his who also became my patient at a later date. Later on, someone who served as a security guard in that prison and later escaped that country told me the same thing. Now there is a book published called *My Life With Salah Nasr* by Imtiaz Kurshid, the mistress of Salah Nasr, chief of Nasser's Intelligence Service 'G15 between 1957 and 1966. She described the techniques used on these political prisons including throwing them in acid tanks, setting them on fire, poisoning them, sexual torture and filming the torture to be enjoyed later by the highest authorities. They say conditions have now improved.

Since 1980, about 250,000 men and women have been arrested for opposing secular dictatorship in Turkey. Recently, a 16 year old girl named Saadet Akkayet was tortured in prison with electric shock applied to her private parts, raped by the security guards for seven hours, then crucified. A 13 year old diabetic boy died in prison of torture. Four small boys died in prison recently. Children are made to watch as their parents are tortured. Instruments of torture include electric shock, kicking, sexual assault, suspension by the wrist or ankle, and insertion into the anus split bamboo sticks (*falaka*). Kurdish minorities have been affected in an even worse way. While the whole world, including the Physicians for Human Rights, confirmed the Iraqi use of chemical weapons which killed thousands of Kurds, the Turkish investigation found no such evidence!

In the uprising of the Muslim brotherhood in 1982 in Hama, about 20,000 were killed by the Syrian Army. Some 2000 prisoners have died in 1986 due to torture. The weapons of torture are classical electric prods to the private parts and mouth, beating, the pouring of scalding and ice cold water alternatively, the insertion of heated metal rods in the rectum of males and repeated rapes of women. In the 1965 uprising in Indonesia, some 25,000 were killed and about 1000 are still jailed and tortured. Many noted scholars have been tortured and killed. The prisons are called Rehabilitation Centers. The techniques used are the same elsewhere.

The brutalities of the Ba'athist Iraqi regime over its Kurdish, Sunni, Shia, and Ikhwan opposition are unsurpassed. Many prominent scholars of both the Sunni and Shia sects and their families have been arrested, tortured and killed in prison. Some 2,500 members of the Muslim Brotherhood and their sympathizers were arrested and tortured in March 1987 for opposing the use of chemical weapons.

In September 1986, the Iraqi Army took 500 Kurdish children between the ages of 12 and 17 hostage. The blood dripping bodies were returned in boxes, and buried in communal graves for which the parents paid 150 dinars each. The use of chemical weapons and the destruction it caused in Kurdish villages on innocent people is now known to the whole world, confirmed by Physicians for Human Rights, in a report called

"Winds of Death." The U.S. State Department is saying now that the reason Libya should not have chemical weapons is because Iraq proved how deadly they can be on civilians. But nobody is asking them who supplied Iraq with chemical weapons and while the Kurds were being killed what were they doing. Even the recent conference in Paris failed to condemn Iraq for its use of chemical weapons.

Practically there is no good news coming out from any Muslim countries about treatment of political prisoners. We know about the recent uprising in Algeria and the way it was crushed, the persecution by Kaddafi of his opponents in exile, the suppression of the Islamic Tendency movement in Tunis, the mass murder of 10,000 Palestinians by the Jordanian Army in the Black September of 1974. Even from Iran, where the Shah and Savak perfected persecution and torture in prison, there are stories now of summary trial and executions of political opponents. If I have missed a Muslim country, it is just due to the length of this paper.

One thing which we wonder about is who is supplying these dictators with the tools of torture? Who trained SAVAK and G15 (of Egypt)? Who sells them electric prods and other weapons of torture to subdue their own people? It is either the CIA or the KGB or one of their collaborators. These dictators are like puppets dancing with their strings tied to their masters in Moscow or Washington They buy machine guns and tanks to fight their enemy-the common people.

All that is going inside the prison in Muslim countries brings us to the subject of oppression or wrongdoing. God is kind and merciful, and has not chosen as His attribute oppressor because He is just. Someone who cis just cannot be an oppressor, nor can He approve of oppression to others. The Quran says: 1. *"God guides not the wrong doers"* (5:19). 2. *"Do not oppress and you will not be oppressed"* (2:279). 3. *"Do not exceed the limit, surely God does not like transgressors"* (5:87). 4. *"Do not think God is heedless of the wrongdoers"* (14:42). 5. *"And those who possess all that is in the earth, and there with as much again, they will verily seek ransom themselves there with on the Day of Resurrection from the awful doom; and there will appear unto them, from their Lord, that where with they never reckoned."* (39:4).

FROM THE SACRED TRADITIONS

Narrated by the Companion Abu Dharr Ghiffari, Prophet Muhammad

(ص) has said that God says: "O my servants, I have forbidden oppression for myself, and have made it forbidden amongst you, so do not oppress one another." Then what seems to be the problem of these dictators who persecute and torture other human beings and fellow Muslims? Their main problem is that they judge others not according to the Quran, but according to their own opinion of what is right and what is wrong. For them, God Almighty says: "*...Those who do not judge what God has sent down are disbelievers (kaffirun)*" (5:44). "*...Those who do not judge by what God has sent down are oppressors (zalimun)* (5:45). "*...Those who do not judge by what God has sent down are evil doers (fasiqun)* (5:46).

And what do these oppressors, evil doers and disbelievers incur upon themselves? "*Lo,—they who persecute believing men and believing women and repent not, theirs will verily be the doom of hell, and theirs will be the doom of burning*" (85:10).

WHAT SHOULD BE DONE?

Islam is a religion of actions tied to beliefs. Muslims are not supposed to be silent spectators of oppression, minding their own way. To be neutral to a scene of injustice, in my opinion, is equal to the continuation of injustice."*And fight them until persecution is no more and religion is only for God. But if they cease, then let there be no hostility except against the wrongdoers*" (2:193). A Tradition says that Prophet Muhammad (ص) advised us: "Whosoever of you sees an evil action, let him change it with his hand, and if he is not able to do so, then with his tongue, and if he is not able to do so, then with his heart, and that is the weakest of faith" (see Muslim on the authority of Abu Said Al Khudri).

What I propose is that in every Muslim country, there should be an internal organization of concerned and conscientious citizens, including physicians, lawyers, educators, and religious scholars who form a united front against such oppression, not to bring down a ruler, but to educate and reform him, to inform the masses, to become better voters and to liberate those innocent people who are still being persecuted in the prisons and to help their families, to inform the world and join the voices of all those who are oppressed into one single cry:

"FEAR GOD AND LET US GO"

"And why should you not fight in the cause of God and for those who being weak are ill-treated and oppressed, men, women and children,

whose cry is 'Our Lord! Rescue us from this town, whose people are oppressors and raise us from You someone who will help us, raise for us from You, someone who will help us" (4:75).

6 REFLECTIONS ON THE EUROCENTRIC VIEW OF HISTORY

Being a physician, it appears that I have been chosen to do the postmortem of the historians from the West. A Eurocentric is defined as a narrow-minded historian of Europe of the past and the present who pays insufficient attention to the scholarship and achievements of the Afro-Asian worlds. It is someone who has a myopic view of history. Such a person does not show sufficient interest in the history of Oriental people. When Malcolm X started studying the Webster dictionary in prison., he noted the word "white" was affiliated with everything good and pure and the word "black" meant everything bad and evil. So he concluded the dictionary must have been written by a white man! The fact is the European textbooks of world history were also written by white men.

Let me begin by giving you some examples from personal experiences. When I told my professor at Indiana University eighteen years ago, that I was from Pakistan, he did not. know where Pakistan was. After I showed him Pakistan on the map. I humbly asked why we in Pakistan know so much about the USA, but even the educated people in this country don't know much about Third World countries. His reply was honest. He said, "Superior nations do not need to know much about the inferior nations except for their trade needs." Twenty years ago, when a professor at the University of Chicago asked me, "How can I tell the difference between an Indian and a Pakistani because they look alike to me" I said,

"You should ask him because I myself cannot tell the difference between a German and an Englishman." I have been in this country for twenty-five years and have been a US citizen for twenty years, but it does not matter. People still ask me where I come from and when I will go back to that place. More recently, a lady in the elevator at the hospital looked at me with curiosity and asked me, "What brought you to this country?" It was Thanksgiving Day and I looked at her with a smile and said, "The same juicy turkey which brought your ancestors to the country."

Before the introduction of civilization in Europe in the 11th to the 16th century. the tribes of Europe lived a primitive life in their dress and manner of eating. and the way they fought wars. It was the educational and cultural exchange that took place during the glorious period of Muslim Spain and subsequent crusades that brought Europe out of the dark agree.

However, Europe never acknowledged the benefits it derived from Islamic culture nor give anything in return. To the contrary, Pope Leo XIII in 1885 "congratulated Christians for having tamed the barbarian nation, bringing them to civility from savagery and for being the leader and teacher of the people." Before that, English poet, Tennyson in 1842, wrote the poem, "Better Fifty Years of Europe than a Cycle of Cathay." Cathay stood for China and he meant that the history of Europe was so important where so many things were happening quickly than the boring. long history of China.

While Europeans looked down on other nations and called them barbarians, backwards, uncivilized, they always had an eye on their fertilized land and products. The expansion of the West was motivated by the hope and profit gained from the trade in spices, rubber, cotton, opium, gold, silver and not the oil. To find "the golden bird" (India) was the desires of every European sailor which finally led Columbus to discover America. Just like the oil wars of these days, those wars were to control the spice. wood, diamonds, and opium trade and other products. After having colonized those countries, they stole everything possible and took whatever they could carry back to their native country, from the Kuh-i Nur diamond to artifacts. The pattern of this imperialistic expansion had camouflaged designs. They would send explorers followed by merchants who would seek businesses. .just like the East India Company, in exchange for treating a princess or other concessions. Then they would send missionaries followed by the armies.

For example out of one chapter in the famous history book, "History Generale" by Alfred Ramfield published in 1892,. there is only one chapter on the Arabs. three chapters on the Ottoman empire, two chapters on India, six chapters on the Far East, and one chapter for the rest of Asia including Iran and other countries. There is one chapter for North Africa and one for the rest of Africa. Now that leaves close to 250 chapters on. Europe itself. Another famous English "universal history" book. has four volumes on Biblical history, eleven on Greek and Roman history. twenty-seven on European history and only fifteen for the whole rest of the world.

Then, the worst thing they did of 100 years of colonial rule was to take away the language and cultural heritage of those countries. They imposed their language on them, that is, the English language on India, the French language on Algeria, and Spanish in South America and through the languages, they controlled the education. William Hunter in 1871 sent a report from India to the British government insisting that English education (without Mohammadan law) be taught to the Muslim youth in India. in order to break Muslim resistance. so that that would be more tolerant. of English rule and eventually accept foreign subjugation. Knowledge is power, the power to dominate. They developed the science of orientalism. Orientalism, as I define it, is the science of knowing the oriental people and their culture in order to subjugate. dominate and enslave them. It is an extension of Western imperialism.

Imperialism by itself is a dominating attitude over a distant society while colonization is the actual settlement and enslaving. It was their desire to create a white empire in far distant places. For example, the creation of Australia from unwanted white people, criminals from England, was a long term desire to create a country of people of their own. White man's desire to rule the rest of the world was met with cultural resistance and sometimes armed resistance. This resistance is still going on and since white people assigned the word "west" to themselves,. it can be best described as the "west and the rest" in the clash of civilizations.

Political slavery became indistinguishable from cultural slavery. Defeated people in colonies looked up to copy the dress of their masters, the language and the ways of their victor. They wanted to behave as their masters after receiving their form of education. Thus, when this colonial master left these countries, they created a class of aristocrats who would act like their master and continue to oppress the real people of those countries. The West's obsession to humiliate the rest of the world did not include just the Arab world, but extended as far as Japan and the Far East.With traditional British eurocentrism, British foreign minister. Sir Earnest Satow, himself in his diary was in conflict with the British imperialism in the 19th century.

If the British had not pursued a policy of racism against Japan, a lasting Anglo-Japanese alliance could have been formed. Similarly, in Africa, the policy of European nations depended on the country they colonized. They evolved the concept of chieftain and now the warlords to the African ruler. Everyone who was not Christian was considered barbarian.

Now let. us examine some of' the eurocentric perceptions or misconceptions in other histories. Take, for example, the history of Medicine It is a well-known fact that between the 9th and the 15th century, Muslim physicians made specific original contributions in Anatomy, Physiology, Pharmacology, Pathology, Microbiology, Surgery and Medicine. They made numerous breakthroughs in the areas of drugs and developed surgical instruments, wrote extensively on diseases, developed vaccines and did operations like tracheotomy. cataract, developed anesthesia and wrote textbook of medicine. The first hospital was. developed in Baghdad in the 11th century and Avicenna's textbook of medicine. *The Cannon* was a textbook in Europe for five centuries. They developed methods to diagnose stomach cancer, measles. smallpox. cholera and the plague. This was all 300 years before bacteriologic discoveries. However. if you read recently published book "history of medicine'; by Lyon and Pettrollis, the extensive achievements of Muslim physicians for eight centuries is described in one paragraph as Arabic medicine and characterized their contributions mainly of "preservation and compilation."

The authors conclude in this book that "certainly the Muslim physicians contributed no original ideas or developed thought, but in the period of unrest (i.e., in the dark ages, they were the preservers of knowledge." There cannot be a worse lie than this because the contributions of Arabic and Muslim physicians is well-preserved to those who do authentic research. Their instruments are well-kept in various European museums. Similarly, Muslim mathematicians developed Mathematics and Algebra which is an Arabic word., Chemistry (which comes from the word alchemy in Arabic), Physics and Astronomy, but if you read modern textbooks of Chemistry, Algebra. and Astronomy. none of the contributions of Muslim scientists are mentioned there. This is a distortion of history.

The second area of distortion of history by eurocentric historians I would like to mention is that of human rights which has been covered extensively in the previous essay.

What needs to be noted here is that not only did eurocentric historians divide the world according to their own needs into the "West" and the "East", "Middle East", "Near-East" and Far-East", the center of the measuring distance being Europe; but they also coined words for other people according to suit their own purpose. So those who sided with them, were called "moderates" or modern. Those who opposed them were called them "fanatics" and "fundamentalists." Sir Winston Churchill called Mr. Gandhi, a leader of 500 million people. "a naked fakir." This is an example of how they perceived the rest of the world. These orientalists like Sir William Muir called Prophet Muhammad an epileptic and a lunatic and the Quran, a forged book. Sir Anthony Eden, the British prime minister, said that "as long as there is the Koran on earth, there can never be peace." How can we forget so much hated and distortion of fact done in the name of scientific, objective research?

Now let me answer some of the myths that the eurocentric historians have managed to inculcate in the minds of the general population.

Islam was spread by the sword: There is no truth to this expression. When Islam was spreading by the sword, what did the non-Muslim army facing the Muslim army have in their hands. Did they have sticks or toothpicks? They also had swords. The sword was the weapon of war at that time. Is it possible that the swords Muslims had in those days were sharper than European swords? There are many places Muslims are in large numbers; for example in Indonesia, many parts of Africa, and China where there is no record of Muslim armies being there. The number of Christians in Japan has increased significantly since World War II. Should we say that in Japan, Christianity is spread by the atom bomb? To say Islam spread by the sword, is to say that Christianity spread by F-16's and Tomahawk missiles, which is not true. The sword of Islam could not conquer all the non-Muslim minorities in Muslim countries. In India where Muslims ruled for 700 years, there is still a minority. And where is the sword of Islam in the US where the Muslims are now over 6 million?

Islam oppresses women: Not true. Islam elevated the status of women 1,400 years ago by giving them the right to divorce, the right to have financial independence and support. and the right to be identified as dignified women at a time when in the rest of the world, including Europe, women had no such rights. In the US alone, about a million women are abused a year by their husbands, boyfriends, or former husbands to the extent that they need to have medical care. Close to five women die a day from such abuses. About 100,000 women are raped every year and only one-third of the rapes are reported. Women are used to market each and every product and they are forced to perform unnatural sex acts as admitted later on by Linda Lovelace. the star of *Deep Throat*. Their bodies in the skin magazines are used to degrade their higher status. In spite of the fact women have been forced to work outside their home, they get much less pay than men of same qualification. In Third World countries (India, Pakistan, Sri Lanka. Bangladesh, Philippines) women can be elected to the highest office, but not in the US. How come, then, that these people who humiliate their own women so much, accuse others of oppressing their women? Does freedom only mean the right to undress in public, the right to kill their infants in their uterus. If this is what liberation means, Muslim women do not want to be part of that.

Muslims have been intolerant of other religious minorities: It is true that sometimes the actions of the ruler does not reflect the teachings of his religion, but in general, Muslims recognize the rights of the minority and Muslim rulers insure their welfare. Prophet Muhammad (ص)forbid Muslim armies to destroy churches and synagogue. Caliph Umar did not even allow the Muslim army to pray inside the church. When in the rest of Europe Jews were persecuted and kicked out, they were welcomed and flourished in Muslim Spain for several hundred years. They considered that a part of their history as their golden era in their 5000 years of history.

In Muslim countries even now, Christians live in prosperity in government positions, attend their church and their missionaries are allowed to operate schools and hospitals. But is the same religious tolerance available to Muslim minorities in non-Muslim countries such as in Yugoslavia or in Israel? Muslims and Jews during the Spanish inquisition were forced to leave the country or become Christian.

All Muslims have four wives: While polygamy is permitted in Islam, in practice there are very few Muslims who have more than one wife. To the contrary, many Western men who claim that they are monogamous, have one wife and more than one affair outside their marriage. Or in their lifetime. they have married several women at different times which is a form of serial polygamy. Historically, all the prophets except Jesus who was not married, had more than one wife.

Islam promotes violence and terrorism: Again, Islam by nature does not do that. Islam condemns all the violence that is sometimes blamed on Muslims and at times is committed by those who have Muslim names. We do not judge Christianity by the violence that happened in the Crusades, the Spanish Inquisition. World War II or the atrocities committed in Bosnia by the Christian Serbs. However, sometimes violence is a human response of oppressed people as it happens in Palestine.

These people have been displaced from their homeland, put in refugee camps and watched their relatives being killed. No one listens to their plight unless they do something to get the attention of the media. Although this is wrong, this is the only way for them to attract attention. There is much terrorism and violence in areas where there is no Muslim presence; for example, in Ireland, South Africa. Latin America and Sri Lanka. Sometimes the violence is due to a struggle between those who do not have the necessities of life or between the oppressed and those who are the oppressors. We need to find out why people become terrorists. Unfortunately, the Palestinians who commit violent acts are called terrorists, but when Tamils in Sri Lanka do the same, they are called rebels.

Arabs are white slave masters: The truth is to the contrary. It was the European nations in Africa who operated most of the slave trade and brought millions of Africans to the United States in ships where so many of them died. They kept them in the Caribbean Islands to torture them and break their will, put them on farms, and changed their name and religion. All of those who have read the book *Roots* know what I am talking about.

The famous missionary teacher, David Livingston, having failed to convert Muslims in Africa to Christianity, wrote that "the Arabs must be forced out of Africa and replaced by Christian missionaries in order to redeem the continent." Slavery was at its peak in Europe in the 15th to the 19th century and as they came out of the Dark Ages and became more civilized, slavery was gradually abolished in Europe and the United States.

Blacks (Afro-Americans) have low IQ and they are violent: Personally, I have known many Afro-Americans who are very intelligent and peaceful people. How can one develop high IQ if he does not get a good education and work experience and is kept busy in drugs, alcohol, music and games? Violence is a reflection of poverty and drug use. After all, all hungry humans are restless. Once their stomach is satisfied, they are peaceful.

Islam is a threat (Muslims are coming): Judith Miller in Spring, 1993 issue of *Foreign Affairs*, writes extensively why she considers (radical) Islam a threat for (the interests of) the Western world.

Orthodox Zionism and Christian Fundamentalism are not a threat to Muslims or even to their own people. Thus I wrote to the editor of *Foreign Affairs* saying that such accusations are a preparation for ethnic cleansing that may engulf England, France, Germany and the USA in the next few decades. The A-bomb by India is not called a Hindu bomb, of Israel is not a Jewish bomb, of England. France and USA is not a Christian bomb, of Russia is not a secular bomb. but the Nuclear Energy Programs of Pakistan and Iran are Islamic bomb!!

Finally, what should be done? It is so painful to read these distortions of history by the writers of the history of the world now that we, the backward people. can read their languages. It is so difficult to re-write the history and undo the past. But historians of today have a role to play irrespective of their religion. The Quran specifically says, *"Oh you people of the Book, cover not the truth with falsehood if you know the truth."*

Now modern historians who do know the truth should write an honest apologetic review of the history and acknowledge the achievements of the oriental people, their culture and achievements and open their hearts and their books for further examination and exchange dialogue. But more importantly, as they write when the history is taking place, for example, in the last twenty years, they should write the truth about the history. For example, who started the Iran-Iraq war? Who supplied Iraq with all of the weapons? Who invited Iraq to invade Kuwait and how Saddam Hussain was made a scapegoat to punish the Iraqi people? How the ethnic cleansing is taking place in Bosnia by the Serbs and their collaborators, the European nations and the United Nations. These things are happening in front of our eyes and if we cannot correct them now, fifty years from now it will be too late and it will be just a matter of academic interest while the history of the world will be changed again in favor of the imperialist. eurocentrism must change to humanocentrism.

7 THE FALLOUT FROM THE CAIRO POPULATION CONFERENCE

S addam Hussain's Scud missiles were more of a nuisance, but their debris falling from their explosions in the air was more damaging. In the same way, the population conference which just ended on September 13, has fallout which may be endangering the whole of mankind, especially those in the Third World, for centuries. If the conference itself was just for discussion, there is no problem. However, it has binding resolutions on which $34 billion will be spent in the next five years to implement its resolutions.

Economic sanctions may be applied on the reluctant Third World countries hopelessly dependent on aid from the USA. and the World Bank. The initial draft resolutions were nothing but a blueprint for the imposition of "condom culture" on the Third World in order to control the population of Muslims, Catholics and other Third World nations. In the words of the Bishop of England, "This is imperialism of the first world over the Third World. The use of the United Nations to impose the new world order on the Third World is deplorable."

The United Nations, traditionally known as a peacemaker, not being able to achieve peace anywhere, has franchised into other ventures now. The Quran, the Muslim holy book, knowing the real intent of these peacemakers, has said, *"They call themselves peacemakers, but indeed they are mischief-makers but they perceive it not"* (2:10). Then Quran instructs mankind, *"Do not cause mischief on earth after it has been set in order"* (7:56).

Although the conference was labeled as a population and development conference, eighty percent of the discussion was on population control only. The same conference held in 1974 and 1984 did not use the word abortion at all.

The United States played a big role, being the condom culture czar, and using the United Nations as its agent. Thus, in March, 1994, when the US. State Department instructed all US embassies to tell their host governments, "The United States believes that the access to safe, legal and voluntary abortion is a fundamental right of all women,"it produced a huge outcry.

This fundamental human right of all women is only in the United States and nowhere else?This is a result of pro-abortion lobby pressure on the US Government. Similarly, in the draft resolution, the inclusion of the word "other unions," next to marriage, was due to pressure from homosexuals and lesbians who recently forced Health Secretary Janet Reno to allow homosexuals to migrate to this country as political refugees seeking asylum if they are persecuted in their own country, as if we have a shortage of homosexuals and AIDS in our country, and we need to import more.

Let us discuss this "real threat" of the population explosion. Two hundred years ago, Malthus predicted that our population growth would be so much that there would be a shortage of food. Then Paul Ehrlich wrote a book, *The Population Bomb*, which is nothing but a masterpiece of propaganda. Many of its predictions have been disproved. The birth rates are actually going down in many areas of the world, both in industrial and in non-industrial countries. Producers of toys, diapers and baby clothes across the United States are diversifying in other fields.

Even if we believe that the world's population in the next thirty years will increase from 5.7 billion presently to 14 billion, that would equal 269 persons per square mile. However, currently, there are 1,140 persons per square mile in the Netherlands, and 848 persons per square mile in Japan. No one is talking about population control in these two countries by using condoms and abortion.

Why are they obsessed with controlling the Third World's population? In a recently declassified US National Security Council document entitled "National Security—Study Memorandum 200" by Henry Kissinger, dated December 10, 1974, the implications of worldwide population growth for US security and overseas claimed that the Third World population growth represented a threat to US national security. There were thirteen key countries that worried him most, and included were Pakistan, Indonesia, Egypt, Bangladesh and Turkey, which constitute a Muslim population of half a billion.

Before him, a US State Department official, Thomas Ferguson, said that population is a political problem, and either they do it "our way, through nice and clean methods, or they will get into the kind of mess we have in E1 Salvador, in Iran or in Beirut." However, this idea of controlling the Third World population even has the philosophical backing from eurocentric philosophers. Several decades earlier, Bertrand Russell said, "The white population of the world will soon cease to grow. The Asiatic races will live longer. The Negroes will live still longer, before their birth rate falls sufficiently to make their number stable without the help of war and pestilence. The less prolific races will have to defend themselves by methods which are disgusting, even if they are necessary.""

Wherever the population control programs have been "successfully installed" under United Nations supervision, it has caused problems. For example, in Indonesia, the birth rate has dropped. However, several women's groups there and in this country denounced their tactics as using excessive social pressure in a repressive manner. Betsy Hartman, Director of Population Studies at Hampshire College, says that the success of the Indonesian program is due to lack of contraceptive choice, authoritarian and pressure tactics, and disregard for women's health.

Let's go to China, where the one-child-per-couple program was successfully implemented. Before the program, the ratio of women to men was nearly equal. Now, since couples are allowed to have only one child, they do gender selection using ultrasound techniques to abort the female child and have only males. Thus, the ratio of men to women is three to one now. Where are these Chinese men going to find women to continue their families in the future?

So the real problem is not current or future overpopulation as much as a problem with mal-distribution, overconsumption and underutilization of much-needed resources. This year the industrialized nations, one-fifth of the world's population, produced nine tenths of all the chlorofluorocarbons, the by-product of all industries which causes pollution and breaks the ozone layer, doing it at the cost of pollution in their own countries as well as in the Third World countries.

The same "promoters of peace and development in the world" are also the sell arms traders, the merchants of death for the Third World. The United States justifiably does not want North Korea, Iran, Pakistan, Libya and Iraq to have nuclear and chemical weapons, but is it prepared to give up some of its own arsenal of weapons of mass destruction? Or have any of the defense producers in the world decreased their exports of conventional weapons to the Third World? No.

Now let us discuss the modus operandi, or the goals of the population conference. In Islam we call it "ways of Satan." The first is universally compulsory sex education. The only two goals of sex education in this country are to prevent teenage pregnancy and to prevent sexually transmitted disease including AIDS. For this they recommended under the umbrella of "reproductive health," that everyone, youth or adult, should have access to condoms and other contraceptive devices. Seventeen billion dollars will be spent to promote this in the next few years, insuring the governments provide "superior quality condoms" to everyone including in the schools and workplaces. But these superior quality condoms have not been able to decrease in the incidence of sexually transmitted diseases or teenage pregnancy of AIDS in this country. How can they do it in the Third World?

The reasons they have failed are three: 1.The AIDS virus is one-third the size of a sperm; therefore, it is permeable . 2.They are expensive and should be used only one time for each act. 3. It takes away the sexual pleasure; therefore, people do not use it as often as they should be using it. However, this emphasis on condom culture will continue, and I would not be surprised if fifteen years from now, my grandchildren would be taught in the alphabet, "C" for condom and "P" for pills.

Their second goal was to undermine the institution of marriage. They wanted women to "delay marriage while continuing to use other methods of contraception while enjoying sex." At the same time, they would encourage women to come out of their houses and compete with men in all the jobs outside. According to them, it is demeaning for women to serve food to their children and their husbands, but to serve food as a waitress in a hotel or as an air hostess for an airline, wearing a miniskirt, is their "empowerment."

Unfortunately, many men, including in this country, will continue to enslave women despite UN. resolutions. The working American women, when they come home, they still have to prepare meals, still have to do the laundry, and still have to do the shopping, while men watch basketball games and drink beer.

Even in this conference of enslavement of women, under the code name of empowerment, heads of the delegations, except for two, were men, and most of the speakers were also men who were telling women not to have families or children but to be available for sex only. Another aim of the conference was to destroy family values which help the Muslims survive. They planned to do this by taking over the rights of the parents from their teenagers by allowing teenagers to have free access to condoms, pills and abortions without the consent or knowledge of their parents.

In the USA., a teenage girl cannot have aspirin from a school nurse without the written approval of the parents, but she can go to an abortion clinic and have an abortion done without the parents' knowledge. Which is more dangerous, aspirin or abortion? At the same time, they ask parents to be financially responsible for their grandchildren born to teenage mothers The breakdown of the family structure and single-parent family is the most serious social problem in the United States, so it wishes the same mess it is i for the rest of the world.

Another aim of the conference was to use abortion as a fertility-regulating agent. The Third World countries will be instructed to have abortions safe and free, available to all those who seek it, or otherwise face sanctions. Their compliance could be strictly monitored and enforced. Mubarak and Bhutto might be told that if you do want US aid, then you have to buy a billion dollars worth of "super-quality condoms" from the USA and the First World, and perform so many abortions per year in your country. The United Nations' supervised genocide in Bosnia and worldwide on fetuses, may have a common goal "to control the population of Muslims."''

THE FINAL DRAFT

The final draft adopted after intense opposition from the Vatican, Latin American countries and Muslims did modify the initial resolution in language. A clause was inserted saying, "Implementation of the document should be consistent with full respect for the various religious and ethical values and cultural backgrounds." The words "marriage and other unions" were changed to "families in various forms." The words "sexual rights" were removed but "reproductive rights of couples and individuals" kept."

After five days of intense negotiation, the Catholics won greater emphasis for passage saying, "Abortion should not be promoted as a means of family planning." The right of migrant family reunification was changed to "the vital importance of family reunification." Emphasis on "empowerment of women" and prohibition of female circumcision stayed in the draft.

What should be our future plans of action? We thank the UN officials who said "fundamentalist Muslims" have collaborated with the Vatican in opposing the population conference. We pray that this understanding between people of faith will continue to prosper to oppose the satanic designs. Muslims and people of faith elsewhere have an obligation to meet this challenge by disseminating the information and educating their own people. They must fight together, arm in arm, against secular immorality and liberal imperialism being imposed on the Third World.

They must develop their own resources and economic growth and not allow the opportunistic, former colonial powers to rob them of their natural resources, or rule their destiny. American people should tell the Clinton administration that it does not need to fight the population of the Third World, but the population and power of the liberal lobby of the coalition of homosexuals and pro-abortion groups.

PART IV:
ISLAMIC MISSIONARY WORK

"Invite (all) to the way of your Lord
with wisdom and beautiful preaching
and argue with them
in ways that are best and most gracious;
for your Lord knows best
who have strayed from His Path
and who receives guidance" (16:125).

1 COMMON MISCONCEPTIONS ABOUT ISLAM

INTRODUCTION

The pluralistic American society is changing from being a "melting pot" to a "salad bowl" in which all ingredients are encouraged to preserve and display their distinct individual taste and flavor. However, even though Islam is a major religion with over I billion followers worldwide and nearly 6 million in the U.S.A., some Americans still think it is a cult, some believe all Muslims are terrorists or have 4 wives, or ask me, if my wife puts on a veil, walks behind me or does belly dancing for me! Thus, the misconceptions about Islam continue because of a lack of correct information about the basic teachings of Islam.

The ongoing crisis in the Muslim world and the misrepresentation of Islam sometimes by the media challenges us to answer questions by our non-Muslim friends about our way of life in a simple and concise language. I have given many lectures to non-Muslim school and college students, church audiences, inter-faith gatherings, and have appeared on radio and TV talk shows. The following responses are based on actual questions asked from me by various non-Muslims with whom I have had contact.

1. WHAT IS ISLAM

The word "Islam" means **peace** and **submission**. Peace means to be at peace with yourself and your surroundings. Submission means to submit to the Will of God. A broader meaning of the word "Islam," is to achieve peace by submitting to the Will of God.

This is a unique religion with a name which signifies a moral attitude and a way of life. Judaism takes its name for the tribe of Judah, Christianity from Jesus Christ, Buddhism from Gautama Buddha and Hinduism from the Indus River. However, Muslims derive their identity from the message of Islam rather than the person of Muhammad (ص) Thus, they should not be called "Muhammadans."

2. WHO IS ALLAH?

This is the Arabic word for "one God." Allah is not the God of Muslims only. He is God of all creations because He is their Creator and Sustainer.

3. WHO IS A MUSLIM?

The word "Muslim" means one who submits to the will of God. This is done by declaring, ""There is no god except the one God and Muhammad is the Messenger of God." In a broader sense, anyone who willingly submits to the Will of God is a Muslim. Thus, all the prophets preceding the Prophet Muhammad (ص) were Muslims. The Quran specifically mentions Abraham, who lived long before Moses and Christ, saying, "He was not a Jew or a Christian, but a Muslim," because he had submitted to the Will of God. Thus, there are Muslims who are not submitting at all to the Will of God and there are Muslims who are doing their best to live an Islamic life. One cannot judge Islam by looking at those individuals who have a Muslim name, but in their actions, they are not living or behaving as Muslims. The state of being a Muslim can be according to the degree to which one submits to the Will of God in his or her beliefs and actions..

4. WHO WAS MUHAMMAD (ص)?

In brief, Muhammad (ص) (peace and the mercy of God be upon him) was born in a noble tribe of Mecca in Arabia in the year 570 AD. His ancestry goes back to Prophet Ishmael (ع), (peace be upon him) son of

Prophet Abraham (ص). His father died before his birth and his mother died when he was six. He had no formal schooling. He was first raised by a nurse as was the custom in those days and then by his grandfather and uncle. As a young man, he was known as a righteous person who used to meditate in a cave. At the age of forty, he was given the prophethood when the angel Gabriel appeared in the cave. Subsequently, the revelations came over a period of twenty-three years and were compiled in the form of a book called the Quran. Muslims consider the Quran to be the final and last word of God. The Arabic of the Quran has been preserved, unchanged, in its original form and confirms the truth in the Torah, the Psalms and the Gospels.

5. DO MUSLIMS WORSHIP MUHAMMAD (ص)?

No. Muslims do not worship Muhammad (ص)or any other prophets. Muslims believe in all prophets including Adam, Noah, Abraham, David, Solomon, Moses and Jesus. Muslims believe that Muhammad (ص).was the last of the prophets. They believe that God alone is to be worshipped, not any human being.

6. WHAT DO MUSLIMS THINK OF JESUS (ع)?

Muslims think highly of Jesus (ع) and his worthy mother, Mary. The Quran tells us that Jesus (ع) was born of a miraculous birth without a father. *"Lo! The likeness of Jesus with God is the likeness of Adam. He created him of dust and then He said to him, 'Be' and he was"* (The Quran, 3:59). He was given many miracles as a prophet. These include speaking soon after his birth in defense of his mother's piety. God's other gifts to him included healing the blind and the sick, reviving the dead, making a bird out of clay and, most importantly, the message he was carrying. These miracles were given to him by God to establish him as a prophet. According to the Quran, he was not crucified, but was raised into heaven (see the Quran, Chapter Mary).

7. DO MUSLIMS HAVE MANY SECTS?

Muslims have no sects. In Islam, there are two major schools of thought, the **Shia** and the **Sunni**. Followers of either group have many things in common. They both follow the same revelation—the Noble Quran. They both follow the same prophet, Muhammad, (ص). They both offer their prescribed prayers five times a day and perform the prescribed fast in the month of Ramadan. Both go at least once in their lifetime on the pilgrimage to Mecca. They both follow Prophet Muhammad (ص)'s sayings and actions, but those who, in addition, follow the sayings and views of 'Ali ibn Abi Talib (the Messenger's first cousin and son-in-law) are called Shia. while those who don't are called Sunnis. Shia means a partisan (party of Ali) and it started more as a political party to help Ali in his conflict with his political adversaries. Most Shias are in Iran and Iraq while the rest of the Muslim world is mostly Sunni. Shias are about 16-percent of the Muslim population.

8. WHAT ARE THE PILLARS OF ISLAM?

There are five major pillars which are the articles of faith. These pillars are:

1) The **belief** (or *iman*) in the one God and that Muhammad (ص) is His Messenger.

2) Prayers (*salat*) which are prescribed five times a day.

3) Fasting (*saum*) which is prescribed in the month of Ramadan.

4) Charity or poor-due (*zakat*) which is the poor-due on the wealth of the rich.

5) Hajj which is the pilgrimage to Mecca once in a lifetime if one can afford it physically and financially.

All the pillars should be of equal height and strength in a building in order to give the building its due shape and proportions. Therefore, all the pillars of Islam should be of similar strength. It is not possible that one would perform the hajj without performing the prescribed fast or without offering the prescribed prayers. Now think of a building which has pillars only. It would not be called a building. In order to make it a building, it has to have a roof, it has to have walls, it has to have doors and windows. These things in Islam are the **moral codes** of Islam which includes honesty or truthfulness, steadfastness and many other human moral qualities. Thus, in order to be a Muslim, one should not only be practicing the pillars of Islam, but should also have the highest possible quality which is possible for a good human being. Only then is the building completed and looks beautiful.

9. WHAT IS THE PURPOSE OF WORSHIP IN ISLAM?

The purpose of worship in Islam is to be God conscious. Thus, the worship, whether it is prescribed prayer, fasting or charity, is a means to an end and the end is consciousness of God so that when one becomes conscious of God in thought and action, one is in a better position to receive His bounties, both in this world and the next.

10. WHAT DO MUSLIMS THINK OF THE HEREAFTER?

God is Just and therefore, in order to show His justice, there has to be a system of accountability. Those who do good have to be rewarded and those who do wrong have to be punished accordingly. Therefore, He created heaven and hellfire and there are admission criteria for each of them. Muslims believe that the present life is temporary. It is a test and if we pass the test, we will be given a life of permanent happiness in the company of good people in heaven.

11. WILL THE GOOD ACTIONS OF THE NON-BELIEVERS BE WASTED?

No. The Quran clearly says, "*Anyone who has done an atom's worth of goodness will see it and anyone who has done an atom's worth of evil will also see it.*" By that, it is meant that those who do not believe, but have done good, will be rewarded in this world for their good deed. On the other hand, those who do good if they are Muslims, will be rewarded not only in this world, but also in the world hereafter as well. However, the final judgment is up to God (The Quran 2:62).

12. WHAT IS THE DRESS CODE FOR MUSLIMS?

Islam emphasizes modesty. No person should be perceived as a sex object. There are certain guidelines both for men and women that their dress should neither be too thin nor too tight to reveal the form of the body. For men, they must at lease cover the area from the knee to the navel. Women's dress should cover all areas except the hands and face.

13. WHAT ARE THE DIETARY PROHIBITIONS IN ISLAM?

Muslims are told in The Quran not to eat pork or pork products, dead animals or the mean of carnivorous animals (because they eat dead animals) nor to drink intoxicants such as wine or use any illicit drugs.

14. WHAT IS JIHAD?

The word "jihad" means struggle or, to be specific, striving in the cause of God. Any struggle done in day-to-day life to please God can be considered jihad. One of the highest levels of jihad is to stand up to a tyrant and speak a word of truth. Control of the self from wrongdoing is also a great *jihad*. One of the forms of *jihad* is to take up arms in defense of Islam or a Muslim country when Islam is attacked. This kind of *jihad* has to be declared by the religious leadership or by a Muslim head of state who is following the Quran and the *sunnah*.

15. WHAT IS THE ISLAMIC YEAR?

The Islamic Year 1 began with the migration (*hijra*) of Prophet Muhammad (ص) from Mecca to Medina in 622 AD. The calendar is based on lunar cycles. A lunar year is 354 days. The first month is called Muharram. 1994 AD is the year 1415 AH in the Islamic calender.

16. WHAT ARE THE MAJOR ISLAMIC FESTIVALS?

Id al-fitr,the Festival marking the end of the month of the prescribed fast in the month of Ramadan, is celebrated with public prayer, feasts and the exchange of gifts. *Id al-adha*, the Festival marking the end of the pilgrimage, is held at the time of annual pilgrimage to Mecca. After congregational prayer, those who can afford to, sacrifice a lamb or a goat to signify Prophet Abraham's obedience to God which he showed by his readiness to sacrifice his son, Ishmael.

17. WHAT IS THE SHARIAH?

The Shariah is the Islamic Divine Law derived from two sources: the Quran and the *sunnah* or Traditions of Prophet Muhammad (ص). It covers every aspect of daily, individual and collective living. The purpose of the Divine Law is to protect the basic human rights of each individual including the right to life, property, political and religious freedom and safeguarding the rights of women and minorities. The law crime rate in Muslim societies is due to the application of Islamic Law.

18. WAS ISLAM SPREAD BY SWORD?

According to the Quran, "There is no compulsion in religion" (2:256). Thus, no one can be forced to become a Muslim. While it is true that in many places where Muslim armies went to liberate people or the land, they did carry the sword because that was the weapon used at that time. However, Islam did to spread by the sword because in many places where there are Muslims now, in the Far East like Indonesia, in China and many parts of Africa, there are no records of any Muslim aries going there. To say that Islam was spread by the sword would be to say that Christianity was spread by guns, F-16's and atomic bombs, etc. which is not true. Christianity was spread by the missionary work of Christians. Ten percent of all Arabs are Christians. The "Sword of Islam" could not convert all the non-Muslim minorities in Muslim countries. In India, where Muslims ruled for 700 years, they are still a minority. In the US, Islam is the fastest growing religion and has six million followers without any swords around.

19. DOES ISLAM PROMOTE VIOLENCE AND
TERRORISM?

No. Islam is a religion of **peace** and **submission** and stresses the sanctity of human life. A verse in The Quran says, *"Anyone who saves one life, it is as if he has saved the whole of mankind and anyone who has killed another person except in case of murder or mischief on earth, it is as if he has killed the whole of mankind"* (The Quran, 5:32). Islam condemns all the violence which happened in the Crusades, in Spain, in WW II, or by acts of people like the Rev. Jim Jones, David Koresh, Dr. Baruch Goldstein, or the atrocities committed in Bosnia by Christian Serbs. Anyone who is doing violence is not practicing his religion. However, sometimes violence is the human response of an oppressed people as is the case in Palestine. These people have been displaced from their homeland, been put in refugee camps, and watched their relatives being killed and no one listens to their plight unless they do something to get the attention of the media. Although this is wrong, they think of this as a way to get attention. There is a lot of terrorism and violence in areas where there is no Muslim presence. For example, in Ireland, South Africa, Latin America, and Sri Lanka. Sometimes violence is due to a struggle between those who have with those who do not have or between those who are oppressed with those who are oppressors. We need to find out why peo-

ple become terrorists. Unfortunately, the Palestinians who are doing violence are called terrorists, but not the armed Israeli settlers when they do
the same.

20. What is "Islamic Fundamentalism?"

There is no concept of "fundamentalism" in Islam. The western
media has coined this term to break those Muslims who wish to return to
the basic fundamental principles of Islam and mould their lives accordingly. Islam is a religion of moderation and a practicing Muslim can neither be a fanatic nor an extremist.

21. Does Islam promote polygamy?

No. Polygamy in Islam is to limit the number of wives. Historically,
all the prophets except Jesus, who never married, had more than one wife.
For Muslim men to have more than one wife is a permission which is
given to them in the Quran, not to satisfy lust, but for the welfare of the
widows and the orphans of war. It is not an injunction. In pre-Islamic
times, men used to have many wives. One person had eleven wives and
when he became a Muslim, he asked Prophet Muhammad (ﷺ), "What
should I do with so many wives?" The Prophet said, "Divorce all except
four." The Quran says, *"You can marry two or three or four women if you
can be equally just with each of them"* (4:3). Since it is very difficult to
be equally just with all wives, in practice, most Muslim men do not have
more than one wife. Prophet Muhammad (ﷺ) himself was married to
only one woman, Khadija, from the age of twenty-five to fifty three. In
western society, some men who have one wife have many extramarital
affairs. A survey published in *USA Today* (April 4, 1988, section D) asked
4,700 mistresses what they would like their status to be. They said that
they preferred being a second wife rather than 'the other woman,' because
they did not have any legal rights nor did they have the financial equality of the legally married wives and it appeared that they were being used
by these men.

22. Does Islam oppress women?

No. On the contrary, Islam elevated the status of women 1,400 years
ago by giving them the right to divorce, the right to have financial independence and support and the right to be identified as dignified women
(wearing the modest dress) when in the rest of the world, including

Europe, women had no such rights. Women are equal to men in all acts of piety (33:32). Islam allows women to keep their maiden name after marriage. Whatever they earn belongs to them alone and they can spend it as they wish. It also asks men to be their protector as women are easily molested. Prophet Muhammad (ص) told Muslim men, "The best among you is the one who is best to his family." Not Islam, but some Muslim men do oppress women today. This is because of their cultural habits or their ignorance about their religion.[1]

23. IS ISLAM INTOLERANT OF OTHER RELIGIOUS MINORITIES?

Islam recognizes the rights of the minority. To ensure their welfare and safety, Muslim rulers initiated a tax (*jaziya*) on them. Prophet Muhammad (ص) forbade Muslim armies to destroy churches and synagogues. Caliph Umar did not even allow them to pray inside a church. Jews were welcomed and flourished in Muslim Span when they were persecuted in the rest of Europe. They consider that part of their history as the Golden Era. In Muslim countries, Christians live in prosperity, hold government positions and attend their church. Christian missionaries are allowed to establish and operate their schools and hospitals. However, the same religious tolerance is not always available to Muslim minorities as seen in the past during the Spanish inquisition and the Crusades or as seen now by the events in former Yugoslavia, Israel and India. Muslims do recognize that sometimes the actions of a ruler doe not reflect the teachings of his religion.

24. WHAT IS THE ISLAMIC VIEW ON:

DATING AND PREMARITAL SEX:

Islam does not approve of intimate mixing of the sexes and forbids premarital or extramarital sex. Islam encourages marriage as a shield to such temptations and as a means of having mutual love, mercy and peace.

ABORTION

Islam considers abortion as murder and does not permit it except to save the mother's life (see Quran 17:23-31, 6:151).

HOMOSEXUALITY AND AIDS

Islam categorically opposes homosexuality and considers it a sin. However, Muslim physicians are advised to care for AIDS patients with the same compassion they give to other patients.

EUTHANASIA AND SUICIDE:

Islam is opposed to both suicide and euthanasia. Muslims do not believe in heroic measures to artificially prolong the life of a terminally ill patient.

ORGAN TRANSPLANTATION:

Islam stresses the saving of lives (see Quran 5:32). Thus, transplantation in general would be considered permissible provided a donor consent is available. The sale of organs is not allowed.

25. HOW SHOULD MUSLIMS TREAT JEWS AND CHRISTIANS?

The Quran calls them the "People of the Book," that is, those who received Divine Scriptures before Muhammad (ص). Muslims are told to treat them with respect and justice and not to fight them unless they initiate hostilities or ridicule their faith. The Muslims' ultimate hope is that they all will join them in worshipping the one God and submitting to His Will.

"Say (O Muhammad): O People of the Book (Jews and Christians), come to an agreement between us and you that we shall worship none but God and that we shall take no partners unto Him and none of us shall take others for Lords beside God. And if they turn away, then say: Bear witness that we are those who have surrendered (unto Him)" (3:64).

2 INVITATION TO AL-ISLAM

❝*Iqra*" or to recite, was the first command of God to Prophet
Muhammad (ص). Several months had passed after the first revelation and no new revelation had come, which made him very
depressed. Then the Surah Al-Mudathir was revealed *"O you wrapped up,
arise and warn."* It was time now that Islam must spread from the first
few, his family, his close friend and his servant to masses in general. The
gift had to be shared with the rest of humanity.

Prophet Muhammad's role has been described in the Quran in many
ways, but the verse which describes his duties in the best way is, *"O you
prophet, we have sent you as a witness, a news bearer, and a warner and
someone who invites people towards to God, by His permission"* (33:45).
His responsibility was also made clear, *"O Messenger, make known whatever has been sent down to you by your Lord and if you do not do so, you
have not conveyed this message"* (5:67).

Thus it became a responsibility for him and for all his followers to
convey the message of Islam. However, his job was not to make people
Muslim, but only to deliver the message. *"It is not required of you (O
Muhammad), to set them on the right path but it is God who guides whom
He wills"* (2:272).

Once we have correctly communicated the message, our obligation is
over. Faith is a seed which God puts in the heart of the believer. It is up
to us to nurture it to a mature plant or suppress it with weeds. After being
given the permission to invite people to Islam, Prophet Muhammad (ص)
was told how to do it. *"Invite (all) to the way of Your Lord with wisdom*

and beautiful preaching and argue with them in ways that are best and most gracious. For Your Lord knows the best, who have strayed away from His path" (16:125). The tools of Islamic Missionary Work are:

CHARACTER OF A MUSLIM PREACHER

The Muslim preacher has to show the example of highest level of character. The Quran could have been placed on the top of mountain and seekers of guidance could have climbed to seek knowledge. What was the need for a prophet. When, after death of Prophet Muhammad (ص), some folks who never met him, came to Ayisha, his wife, and asked her to describe his character, she asked, "Have you not read the Quran?" When they said they had, she continued, "He was a living example of the guidebook revealed to him. *"Verily in the messenger of God, you have a good example who looks towards God and last day and mentions God many times"* (33:21). The Prophet himself has said, "I have been sent to perfect your moral conduct."

BELIEF IN THE PRODUCT

A Muslim preacher has to have highest and strongest level of faith in God in his or her heart which is reflected in his or her actions. There is no way a preacher can convince others about the product (*islam*) if he or she has some doubts in himself or herself about it. That is why a preacher has to strengthen his or her faith first before he or she sets out for missionary work as he or she may be faced with people who will put questions in his or her mind.

KNOWLEDGE OF ISLAM

This is essential especially from the Quran and *sunnah*. The Muslim preacher should know the Quran; if not by memory, then he or she should be able to know, i.e., what section deals with divorce, wine, etc. He or she should make his or her own notebook. A Muslim preacher should know the major Traditions, especially the situation of how the Prophet dealt with certain situations. He or she should also be versed in other religions so as to give a comparative analysis. He or she should be armed with the knowledge of The Quran and whatever else be needed; i.e., Knowledge of Science and Medicine to engage in intelligent scientific Islamic discussion.

PERSISTENCE IN MISSIONARY WORK

This is very crucial to success, never give up. Even if you spend all your life, never lose hope for Mercy of God. Even prophets were not successful in some areas, Noah for his son, Abraham for his father, Lot for his wife, Muhammad for his uncle. And when Jonah lost hope and left his folks out of despair, he was punished by God, so the message is keep doing what you are doing irrespective of rejection, but ask God for help. Let us discuss some of the qualities of a Muslim preacher.

Muslim Preachers are Teachers

They teach Islam to the ignorant. Good teachers never gets angry at their students, but encourages them even in their weakness. Teachers have to do lots of hard work and have patience. That is why in Surah al-Asr, patience is stressed, since without patience one cannot teach the Truth. And again, teachers have to have good knowledge of the subject.

Muslim Preaches are Soldiers

Soldiers are always ready, so should Muslim preachers be because this is a full time job. Soldiers are always armed, so should be and should arm Muslims with knowledge of Islam (the Quran and *sunnah*). Soldiers have a mission in life, so should Muslim preachers. The purpose of life on this earth is to establish God's religion.

Muslim Preachers are Salespeople

Muslim preachers are a salespeople, smiling and sweet-talking salespersons. If salespersons fight and argue with the customer, do you think people will buy the product. Salespersons are also persistent and never satisfied until they have sold the product. Good salespersons are the one who provides service for the product after they sell it. Thus, Muslim preachers should continue to look after the customer. Good salespersons are friendly, so should Muslim preachers be friendly. "*God has purchased of the believers, their persons and their goods, for theirs (in return) is the garden (of Paradise)*" (9:111). Good salespersons should continue to service the product. As a result of our missionary work and guidance from God, if one becomes a Muslim, do we follow-up with that person? Do we help that person and support him or her in remaining a Muslim?

Muslim Preachers are Physicians

Like physicians, they should be able to diagnose the illness in the heart of unbeliever/disbeliever and be able to prescribe a remedy in an appropriate dose. They know the medicine is *"Oh mankind! there has come to you direction from your Lord and a healing for the disease in your heart for those who believe in guidance and mercy"* (10:57).

PROBLEMS OF ISLAMIC MISSIONARY WORK

Just as Islam is spreading in non-Muslim countries, Christianity is spreading in Muslim countries by two different methods. While we have a better product, they cater better to humanitarian needs of the poor and destitute in Muslim countries, which should have been our priority to begin with. Christian missionaries are spending thousands and millions of dollars in Muslim countries in relief work, in establishing schools, colleges and hospitals. Are rich Muslim countries and individuals doing the same in non-Muslim countries? Most of the leaders of Muslim countries were educated in a missionary or western school. Thus taking care of the poor, the sick, the widow and orphan is and should be part of Islamic missionary work to non-Muslims.

Similarly, missionary work in the prisons need re-evaluation. Out of 1,000,000 inmates in this country, 200,000 are Muslims who entered prison as non-Muslims, but received guidance while serving. Their needs are more than lectures, books and brochures. They are human beings. Their families usually abandon them when they accept Islam. Someone needs to write to tell them: We love you and when you come out, we will help you re-enter the society and give you financial and social support.

Through "The Quran Account," a charitable organization for education, we have helped 4,000 of them in the last 10 years by providing them such support along with educational tools. We also need to fight for their Islamic rights of having permissible food, time for performing the prescribed fast, Friday congregational prescribed prayer, etc. If we do not absorb them into society, most likely they will go back to crime, prison and to disbelief.

The obstacles to the efforts of missionary work are not from the CIA, US. Government, or evangelists, but from we Muslims, in showing Islam in its true meaning and example: a) the secular Muslim who may be a good human being, but is devoid of rituals of Islam nor he can identify himself with Muslim cause, b) the traditionalist who does all rituals and details of *sunnah,* but does not know the philosophy of Islam. He has not come out of the first 100 years of Islam and cannot relate to problems of modern society. They have good intentions but not "the beauty and wisdom of beautiful preaching." While the second category is not fit to give missionary work, the first one himself is most deserving of our attention.

3 WHAT IS REQUIRED OF US AS MUSLIMS?

In order to become a legal Muslim, all we have to do is to say the two statements in Arabic "There is no God except God, and Muhammad is His Messenger." Once we have said it three times, knowing and accepting the meaning of it, we are Muslim for all practical and legal purposes (i.e., marriage, inheritance, etc.). However, bearing witness to this is not enough to lead a life of Muslim. Saying these statements can be compared to, say, joining the army by applying and wearing the uniform. However, in order to remain a GI, one has to learn to fight and fight when unnecessary

WHAT DO THE STATEMENTS MEAN?

When we say, "There is no god except," we are denouncing all false gods within and around us in whatever shape they were and in whatever ways we worshipped. So not only we are denouncing idols but anything we thought would benefit us or hurt us except One God, God. Thus, if we feared the powers of a human or say we worshipped wealth, we have to denounce that. Now that we said our belief in One God, God, we have to believe in Him with All His Majesty, All His Powers, and All His Beautiful Names (many of which are mentioned in the Quran). So when we are saying this statement, we are actually saying that, for example, there is no one more compassionate and merciful (*rahman* and *rahim*) than God, there is no one more Wise, more Knowledgeable, more Forgiving, and more Trustworthy than Him, and so on.

151

Then when we say that Muhammad is the Messenger of God, we are affirming our belief in the Quran, as the word of God, since the Quran came to us through Muhammad (ص). He not only taught what was revealed to him from God, but also lived a life translating the Quran into his personal actions. A group of Muslims came to Ayisha, wife of Prophet Muhammad (ص) after his death and asked, "We never saw the Prophet in person, tell us how was his personality?" Her reply was simple, "Have you not read the Quran? He lived by it." So belief in the message (the Quran) is part of belief in the Messenger.

Faith is like a seed which God puts in the heart of whoever He wishes. Then all that person can do is to nourish the plant that grows out of that seed into a strong fruitful tree or let it be subdued by the weeds (bad actions) and die. Like a tree where roots are submerged in the ground and the tree is on the top, the part of faith is in the heart and the other parties expressed on the tongue and in the actions. Thus our actions become the expression of our faith (or lack of it).

Faith also includes belief in all the prophets of God, from Adam to Muhammad, all the books these prophets were given as books of God, the angels of God, the Day of Judgment, life after death, the unseen like heaven and hell, and that God has knowledge and power to execute all His plans..

EXPRESSION OF FAITH WITH ACTIONS

The major application of faith is what we call the Pillars of Islam. They include prescribed prayer (*salat*),prescribed fasting (*saum*), Charity (*zakat*), and pilgrimage to Mecca (*hajj*). However, *salat, zakat, saum* and *hajj* are entities in themselves and cannot be simply translated as above.

PRESCRIBED PRAYER

These are the five prescribed prayers which are performed early in the morning (before dawn), at noon, in the afternoon, at sunset, evening and preferably (but not a must), in the late hours in the night. Before each prescribed prayer, one has to have external and internal purity. These include ablution, purity of cloth and ground used for the prescribed prayer, proper and clean clothing, declaring one's intention, and facing the Kabah at Makkah (*qiblah*). Bowing down and prostration are acts of surrender. The prescribed prayer is to communicate with one's Creator and bring one closer to Him.

PRESCRIBED FAST

The prescribed fast (except for those who are, i.e., travelers, sick, children, menstruating and nursing women) is in the month of Ramadan from dawn to dusk, abstaining from food, drink and sex.

POOR-DUE

The poor-due or charity (*zakat*) is the right of the poor over the wealth of the rich. Anyone who has at the end of a year a certain wealth accumulated, must give 2.5% as charity to purify his or her legal wealth. He or she can give more then if he or she wishes. No one is exempt from the poor-due except one who does not have any excess wealth.

PILGRIMAGE TO MECCA

Pilgrimage (*hajj*) to Mecca is not a sight-seeing trip to the Holy Places. It is a worship in the tradition of Prophet Abraham, for everyone once in his/her lifetime if he/she can afford it financially and physically. It is the annual assembly of Muslims from all over the world. The usual number is between two and three million, all dressed in white unsewn cloth.

JIHAD

There is one additional pillar which is called *jihad*. It is wrongfully translated by Western writers as Holy War. The actual translation and meaning of *jihad* is striving with everything available in the cause of God. The *jihad* of the self in trying to control our desires is the greatest *jihad* as described by Prophet Muhammad (ﺹ). Thus, in order to wake-up at dawn to perform the prescribed prayer, to fast in the month of Ramadan, to give part of one's money to the poor, to undergo the hardship of the pilgrimage; all are *jihad*. When a Muslim nation is attacked by non-Muslims, then to stand up and fight with one's person or wealth is also a *jihad*.

No building is called a building which has only four or five pillars. You need a roof, walls, doors, etc. These are the moral codes of Islam as expressed in pure actions, for the pleasure of God. In the Quran at 127 places where Heaven is rewarded to the believers,faith is tied to pure actions. These pure deeds have to be expressed in one's personal family, social, economical, political, and spiritual life and require consciousness of God (*taqwa*), constantly and willingly, in order to receive His pleasure and avoid His displeasure.

FEATURES OF BELIEVERS
AS DESCRIBED IN THE QURAN

In Surah al-Mu'minun, they are described as those who are humble in their prayers, avoid vain talk, pay poor-due, and guard their modesty. In In Surah al-Infal, they are described as those who feel fear in their heart when God is mentioned and their faith increases when the Quran is being recited. They trust in their Lord, who establishes worship and gives poor-due. In Sura Tawba, they are mentioned as those who protect each other, enjoin right and forbid what is wrong, and they strive in the way of God. In Surah Rad, they are described as those who have patience, who keep their trust, migrate for the sake of God, and do what they say. In Surah al Hujurat, they are told to speak in a low voice, avoid gossip, rumors, ridicule, defaming or giving offensive name, avoid suspicion, spying and backbiting and make peace between believers. We should reflect upon ourselves and ponder how much of the contract and job description we are maintaining in our lifestyle.

4 JUDAISM, CHRISTIANITY AND ISLAM: CAN THEY PEACEFULLY CO-EXIST TOGETHER?

I want to take up the question being asked today in 4 sections.

a. Is there a theoretical basis for such co-existence?

b. Has there been examples of peaceful co-existence in the past?

c. Why is there so much hostility that makes us ask this question now?

d. What should be done?

Judaism, Christianity and Islam are referred in Islam as the Abrahamic faiths. Prophet Abraham is considered the father of these three religions. We Muslims believe in all prophets to include Moses, Jesus and Muhammad as messengers of God and essentially carrying the same message i.e. to believe in one God, do good and avoid wrong. We have a special place for Jews and Christians and the Quran refers to them as the"People of the Book" i.e. those who received Holy Scriptures—the Pentateuch and the New Testament—before the Quran was revealed. There is a common call for them. "*Say; O People of the Book! Come to an agreement between us and you, that we shall worship no God except one God, and that we ascribe no partners unto Him, and none of us shall take others for Lords beside one God, and if they turn away, than say: I bear witness that we are they who have surrendered unto Him)*" (3:64-65).

Muslims are asked to follow the good examples of earlier prophets. *"In the matters of faith, He has ordained for you that which He had ordained upon Noah, and unto which we gave you (O Muhammad) insight through revelation as well as that which had enjoined upon Abraham, Moses and Jesus. Steadfastly uphold the faith and do not break up your unity"* (42:13).*"Among the people of the book there are upright people, who recite God's messages, throughout the night and prostrate themselves (before Him). They believe in God, and the last day, and enjoin the doing of what is right, forbid what is wrong and vie with another in doing good work, these are among the righteous and whatever good they do, they shall never be denied the reward thereof, or God has full knowledge of those who are conscious of Him"* (3:113 - 115).

It is for this reason that we are advised in the Quran to deal with people of the Book with special status. Their food has been made lawful to us, and marrying their women has been allowed (the Quran 5:5), and we are told *"Do not argue with the people of the Book otherwise than in most kind manner..."* (29:46).

EXAMPLES OF PEACEFUL CO-EXISTENCE IN THE PAST

There are numerous examples. Even in the days of Prophet Muhammad (‎ﷺ) he used to ask his wife to remember her Jewish neighbor in their meal. Once he stood up for the funeral of a Jew. He allowed Christian delegation from Najran to stay *in* the mosque and pray there. He forbade Muslim armies to destroy churches and synagogues as prohibited in the Quran (22:40). He advised Muslims to emigrate to Christian Abyssinia to enjoy the justice of Christian monarch there. He freed the daughter of Hatim, the ruler of Christian tribe Tayyi.

With Jews we have a long history of peaceful co-existence. When Jews were being persecuted in Europe in the Middle Ages, where did they find peace and harmony? It was Muslim Spain, It is that era of Jewish history that they call the "Golden Age". As Rabbi Minken put it, "it was Mohammedan Spain, the only land the Jew knew in centuries after their dispersion which made the genius of physician **possible**." After the fall of Spain, they followed Muslims to Morocco and to Egypt where Maimonides became the personal physician of Saladin, who sent him to King Richard to treat the king. In the Ottoman Empire, Jews and Muslims lived and flourished together. Muslim scholars always respected the rights of **non**-Muslim minority. When the Mongol Tartar became Muslim after capturing Baghdad, he wanted to free fellow Muslims, but Ibn Taimiyyah insisted that the king, if he was a true Muslim should free non-Muslim prisoners, too. It was the generosity of the Muslim Mogul Emperor of India which allowed the operation of the East India Company which later on colonized India.

Islam spread like a wildfire because of its message of peace, submission, brotherhood and equality. As a Muslim soldier, Rabi Ibn Amir, put it, "God sent us to get people out of enslaving one another, into worshipping equally the one God, out of hard and narrow living into an easier and wider one, out of injustice of the absolute power of the ruler into the justice of restricted authority in Islam." It is for this reason, not swords, that Islam is still spreading fast in the West again. Both Islam and Christianity are missionary religions, although in Islam there is no organized clergy.

Those who portray Islam as a religion promoting hate, violence and bloodshed have neither read the Quran or the Traditions in depth. They pick up one or two verses of the Quran and use it to express their own hatred of Islam and Muslims. We Muslims are to respond only to hostility in self defense. To pacify them I quote directly from the Quran. *"God only forbids you to turn in friendship towards such as those who fight against You because of (your faith) and drive you forth from your homeland, or aid (others) in driving your forth"* (60:9). *"O you who believe! Take not as intimate friends such of those who received the scripture before you, and of disbelievers, as those who make fun of Your ? But keep your duty to God if you are true believers"* (5:57). And, *"Whoever kills a human being, not in lieu of another human being, or because of mischief on earth, it is as if he has killed all mankind, and if he saves a human life, he has saved life of all mankind"* (5:32).

WHY THERE IS SO MUCH HOSTILITY NOW?

There are many reasons. To begin with, are is the differences in belief. Both Judaism and Islam do not consider Jesus as God, son of God or mediator between man and God. For this Jews had to pay a heavy price in Europe at the hand of Christians. Muslims paid during the Crusades. While we Muslims believe in Moses and Jesus, they i.e. Jews and Christians never accepted Muhammad (ص) as the last Prophet and the Quran as the last word of God. Some of them even called Muhammad a epileptic and covertly supported those who attacked Islam and Muhammad under freedom of speech. But same freedom was never extended to those who lied otherwise i.e. denied the occurrence of Holocaust.

I agree there has been lot of bloodshed between the three religions, but the same has occurred among themselves too. In the WWII alone nearly 20 million Jews and Christians killed themselves.

Why are the Christians fighting among themselves in Ireland and in Lebanon? The real conflict in the world today is not between religion but between oppressor or oppressed, between those who have and those who have not. Why there is so much unrest and bloodshed in places where Islam is not a factor i.e. Korea, South Africa, Central and South America?

Islam is not passive, but a living and dynamic religion. It is opposed to injustice and oppression. We don't believe in peace and tranquillity as it reigns over the graveyard of Normandy and Hiroshima. We are for peace with honor and peace with justice. Muslims are to help those who are oppressed. It is for this reason that Christians of Lebanon opposing the army of General Aoun, seek shelter in Muslim west Beirut now.

Muslim countries after 200 years of colonial rule are waking up and realizing what they were robbed of during those years, everything from minerals, diamonds to their lead in education and sciences, to their self esteem. Thus they are struggling to regain their past glory. They have been made refugee in their own homeland, exiled from their birth places, and no one wants to listen to their genuine demands. The only thing which gets attention of the media is violent acts.

They call themselves freedom fighter we call them terrorist, but what is the difference between state sponsored terrorism carried by F-16's and school boys throwing stones, just degree of magnitude? The Quran demands we fight oppression, "*...and why should you not fight in the cause of God and for those who being weak are ill treated and oppressed, men, women and children, whose cry is 'Our Lord! Rescue us from this town, whose people are oppressors and raise us from you someone who will help us, raise for us from you someone who will help us'*" (the Quran, 4:75).

WHAT SHOULD BE DONE?

We should learn to know each other. It has been said "The human being is the enemy of what he does not know and whom he does not know." *"O humanity! Lo we have created you male and female and have made you natives and tribes that the noblest of you, is the best in conduct. Lo! God is Knower, Aware"* (49:13).

It through such mutual dialogues or trialogue that we can come together. In Islam, *"There is no compulsion in religion"* (2:256). Differences do not mean hostilities. We should accept each other as fellow human beings and creations of the same one God. We should recognize the rights of the minority. It is the minority which needs the protection of the state. The majority can protect itself. Finally we should neither approve or support oppression, but do our best to undo the injustice done in the past. Only then, after we win over the heart of the others, then we can live in peace. All over the world these three religions are realizing the need for peaceful co-existence so that we can divert over resources in-helping our people. We need to support such dialogues and caring together for the pleasure of our creator.

5 Malcolm X: The Prince of Islam in North America

When Malcolm X became El-Hajj Malik El-Shabazz in 1964, I was a medical student in a Muslim country where the media was controlled by the West. It portrayed him as a Black, militant leader, preaching hate and violence, deviating from the religion of peace and submission. Thus, when I arrived in the USA in 1969, I hardly knew the true nature of this great Muslim leader. For the next twenty years, my state of ignorance remained, although my knowledge of him had improved, collected in bits and pieces. In 1988 a friend recommended his biography to me written by Alex Haley. I bought the book, glanced through it, then gave it to my teenage daughter, who read it cover to cover. Then she suggested that I read it fully, but still I did not,although by then, I had begun to understand and appreciate him a little bit better. Then, strangely a year ago, Malcolm X appeared in my dream. I could not understand why? In the movie there is a scene toward the end, when after returning from Makkah, he is announces the formation of a new organization. He is sitting on a stage with several others. I saw that section of the movie in my dream. He looked at me and smiled. Several weeks ago, I found a copy of a 1989 issue of *Message International*, an Islamic publication from New York, with a cover picture of Malcolm X. There were many articles about him inside, but strangely I found inside an article by me in the same issue. What an honor for me. I know now why he smiled at me in the dream. I hope that I will be in the company of this great martyr in the life hereafter (*amin*).

Malcolm X has now touched me personally and my children. My 12-year-old son, Ahmad, saw the movie, felt proud to be a Muslim, and asked me to lend him the biography. Then he went to his principal and said, " I am a Muslim and I want to start doing noon prescribed prayer in school." Dr. Wilson, a great educator, gave him the permission after requesting a note from his parents, which we gave him. Now, Ahmad is the only Muslim student in his school who does daily noon prescribed prayer on time. Masood, my teenager, became sad after seeing the movie and said, "Look Dad, when he started to do something about Islam, they killed him". I told him that he is not dead, quoting the verse from the Quran, *"And call not those who are slain in the way of God dead, nay they are living, only you perceive not"* (2:154). I told him that he may not be with us now, but he has left you and me and many other Muslims to carry on his mission. Now Masood does regular prescribed prayers and started to grow a nice beard. He replaced his L.A. Knight inverted cap (black) to a white *kufi*. A year ago Masood had won my heart by going to his principal and requesting that the boys rest room in the school should have doors as we Muslims need privacy. His principle was so impressed that he put doors on all the rest rooms.

ANALYSIS OF THE MISSION OF MALCOLM X

Islam erases the past as it did that of Umar ibn al-Khattab, the second rightly-guided caliph. In Islam it does not matter where or how you begin your journey.What matters is the direction you are travelling, with what intention and where you end your journey. Thus the Tradition of Prophet Muhammad (ﷺ) goes like this: There was a man who had committed ninety-nine murders, but his intention was to be purified and be forgiven, so he went to a scholar and asked him if there was a chance for him after committing so many murders, to be forgiven. The scholar said "No, your sins are too many to be forgiven." Out of despair, the man killed the scholar too, but his heart was not satisfied. He went to another scholar and asked the same question. This scholar said, "You are living in a society where you are doing these crimes because everyone else is doing such crimes. There is no hope for you unless you leave this society and go to the next city, in which there is pious people living and you live with them and it will be hoped that you will become a good person, give up committing murder, ask for forgiveness and you will be forgiven."

The man understood the point and started his journey toward the city of the good people. He died on the way there. The angel from hell came down to claim the soul of this man and so did the angel from heaven, and they were arguing. A third person passed by who asked these two angels,who were arguing among themselves,why they were fighting. The angel from hell said, "This man has died and I have been told to claim his body because he has not done any good in his life and he has committed about 100 murders." The angel from heaven said, "Although this man has been sinful throughout his life, he had repented and wanted to become good. He was on a journey to the city of good people so that he could live among them and be forgiven. Therefore, since his intention was good, he belongs in heaven." The man said, "Let's settle this dispute by measuring the distance from the city he left to where he died and from where he died to the city he was going to. If he is closer to the city that he left, he should go to hell and if he is closer to the city he was going to, then he should go to heaven." The angels measured the distance and found him to be closer to the city he was going to and he was taken to heaven. The story closed.

From the life and struggle of Malcolm X, we learn that after becoming a legal Muslim, by taking the words of bearing witness to the One God and the prophethood of Muhammad (ص), we must strive to become a practical Muslim by continuing to seek the true knowledge and the truth. Once we discover it, it becomes binding on us to practice it, before we can preach it. Thus we see that Malcolm X, once he discovered the true nature of Islam, he was fascinated by it and denounced all false previous notions he had in his press conference upon returning to the USA after his pilgrimage.

The second lesson we learn from his life is that Muslims should stand up to oppression and injustice. Islam is not a religion which preaches peace by tolerating injustice and oppression. In fact, the greatest *jihad* is standing up to a tyrant and saying a word of truth. Most of us live in a conspiracy of silence with our establishment. We are afraid to rock the boat in order to preserve the peace. When the leaders of Quraysh asked the Prophet (ص) for a compromise, to allow them to have their idols in the Kabah, and in return they would let Muslims preach Islam, Surah al-Kafirun was revealed. What Malcolm X did to Elijah Muhammad, his mentor, was one of the greatest *jihad*s of our time on an individual level.

He gave his life, opposing adultery and hypocrisy, while many of us do not have the strength to do so and accept this deviation as a normal way of life in the society as we have accepted homosexuality.

I liked his comparison of the house slave versus the farm slave. As he said in his interview, the house slave lives in the house of the master, gets his leftover food, sleeps comfortably and then tries to please his master whether the master is right or is wrong. In reward the master lets him have some concessions and some comforts of life. On the other hand, the farm slave who lives under the difficult conditions of weather and hardship on the farm, is subjected more to oppression and therefore, once he speaks his mind, he is severely punished. Most of us in our own life are very close to being a house slave as we do not stand up and speak to the oppressor for the fear of losing some of our privileges. Malcolm X was strong enough to admit his past mistakes. Many of us live in the life of secrecy of our past and insist on justifying our wrong actions and words, never to admit guilt and repent or ask for forgiveness.

He was invited by his Creator to visit His house in Mecca. After the pilgrimage, a Muslim can have one of the two best things happen to him. a.) To live a life of righteousness thereafter for the rest of his life. b.) Not to live long enough in this world full of temptations and sins. Malcolm X met both criteria and thus there was no need for him to stay on this earth. His mission was now complete.

However, our mission has not even started yet. The message of Islam has not reached most of non-Muslims in its correct form. We Muslims ourselves are plagued with racism which manifests in our pride, in our ethnic origin, color and language. And even in the form of our silence to wrong-doing and oppression. Sometimes this manifests even in the form of pride in our piety and Islamic work.

As the children in the movie said, "We are all Malcolm X." In a sense, we are all influenced to some degree by the evils of the society in which we live. We are either victims or perpetrators of racism and oppression, and sometime a hypocrite in what we say we believe in and we preach and what we practice in our personal life. The question is when and how we will come out of the state of Malcolm X to be purified by our Creator and become El-Hajj Malik El-Shabazz, the prince of Islam in North America. May God be pleased with him and accept his *jihad.* *"Oh you soul at peace, return to thy Lord, content in His good pleasure. Enter you among My bondsmen, enter you My garden"*(89:27-30).

6 TAKING ISLAM AND MUSLIMS OUT OF THE CLOSET: PRACTICAL GUIDELINES

During the early days of Islam, Muslims were so weak that they had to perform the prescribed prayer inside their house for the fear of the persecution that they would receive if they identified themselves as Muslims. It was during those days that Ibn Masud, one of the Companions, was brave enough and wanted to recite the Quran near the Kabah. The Messenger of God (ص) had warned him that he might get beaten up but he went anyway and recited the Quran to the unbelievers who were initially stunned by listening to the recitation of the Quran. At the end, the disbelievers realized what he was doing and became angry and started to beat him. When he returned to the Prophet, the Prophet said, "Did I not warn you before?" He replied, "I will be more than happy to go back and do the same thing even if I get beaten up again."

That was the strength of the beliefs of Muslims those days, during that period of weakness of Islam, The Messenger did pray to God to grant Muslims a strong leader among the unbelievers and he prayed specifically for two of the them; one was Umar and the other was Abu Jahl.

Since Abu Jahl's fate was sealed as an unbeliever, Umar was selected who, being one of the strong leaders of the committee, was very powerful. Now once Umar became a Muslim, he declared that now that now that he was a Muslim, Muslims do not have to perform their prescribed prayers inside their house. They can come out and perform the prescribed prayer in congregation and he would stop anyone who opposed them.

It appears that the attack that the media and other enemies of Islam have launched against Muslims by calling them terrorists, hijackers, backward, fanatics, fundamentalists, etc., has put many Muslims in a defensive position. Some of these people are unable to identify themselves as Muslims or with Muslim causes. They may be good in practicing Islam individually in their homes, but not strong enough to do so collectively in public.

There was a Muslim in our community who seemed to be a tiger in the mosque, but when I asked his fellow worker, who is a non-Muslim, how this person was doing,, his fellow worker, who is a patient of mine, was surprised to learn this tiger was a Muslim because he had never identified himself as a Muslim and each time the talk on Islam would come in the office cafeteria, he would keep quiet for the fear of being identified as a Muslim. It is happening to some of our children also who do not wish to be ridiculed as Muslim when they identify themselves in the schools. So Islam, in the USA has become a religion which is being preached from minarets, being taught in Sunday schools, being shown in Islamic convention bazaars, and in Islamic magazines, but the Muslim presence which is equal to or more than Jews is hardly seen in mainstream public life.

But thank God, the situation has much improved since I came to this country a quarter of a century ago Non-Muslim institutions are becoming sensitive and aware of the needs of Muslims. There was a time, many years ago, when Muslim meals were not available in air flight by airlines and when one would ask the question "why," the airline would say "since their is no demand." Now, when I call for reservations, I say, "Do you have a Muslim or kosher meal?"and many airlines say, "We have both, which one would you prefer."

Again, this is due to the fact that we are becoming more bold and able to identify ourselves as Muslims. More Muslim women are wearing the modest dress. More Muslim young men are growing beards. Sometimes Muslims are walking around in public places with their traditional dress and caps.

I will give you some practical examples from my own personal experience. In New York at a hotel where I was staying, I ordered a plain omelet for breakfast. The American waitress looked at me and said, "Would you like to order something else as this has ham and I am sure you are a Muslim. I know Muslims don't eat pork or ham." I was very pleased with her and I thanked God for making me look like a Muslim.

I received an invitation to attend an Interfaith conference which was basically run by Jews and Christians. I write back to that organization which was the Indiana Commission for Interreligious Equality, saying that I could not attend this conference since they did not have a Muslim speaker or a topic on Islam. They realized their mistake and wrote me, saying, "Yes, we would like to have Muslim participation and would like Muslims to join the board of IICHE." The same Jewish-Christian conference has now become Jewish-Christian-Muslim conference.

Recently I had the experience of organizing Friday prescribed congregational prayer in a non-Muslim convention which I would like to share. When there is a Muslim convention, we should have our own rules and prayer room and prayer times, but it had never occurred to me in the past that this could be done in a non-Muslim medical convention. So when I registered for this convention of internal medicine specialists, 1,200 of them in New Orleans, the first thing which struck me was that on Friday, there was only a one hour lunch break which was not enough time to go to any mosque in the city and get back in time to start the meeting. I thought that perhaps I should just perform the Friday prescribed prayer by myself in my room.

Then it occurred to me that maybe there were other Muslim physicians and that we could organize a Friday congregational prescribed prayer in this hotel. I picked up the phone and called the manager of the hotel and said that I was a Muslim. I said that there were other Muslim doctors attending this convention and we would like to offer a Friday prescribed congregational prayer which is done at 1 o'clock and we would like to have a room to do so. To my pleasant surprise, he said, "Yes, we would love to do it for you. Just tell us how many people are coming and what are your needs." So I went through the names of registered physicians and found that there were thirty-five Muslim physicians from all over the country who had come to attend this particular convention. I told the assistant manager that we had about thirty-five people and we did not need any furniture, to just put plain white sheets on the floor and that is all we need and he agreed to do that.

Then the job was how to find these physicians and give them the message. I did three things: 1) I made up a flyer of the time and room location of this and asked the bell captain to put in the rooms of these physicians, 2) I put a message on the notice board of the convention and 3) I had one of the speakers announce before starting the session Friday morning for those Muslim physicians who planned to perform the Friday congregational prescribed prayer at 1 o'clock to go to such and such room.

This announcement as well as the flyer going to the room was taken with a pleasant surprise by all the Muslim physicians. Ninety percent of them came for the Friday prayer. We shortened the sermon and performed the Friday prayer along with afternoon prayer afterwards in congregation. I felt very good about it and all of the Muslim physicians thanked me and I thanked God. This shows an example that if you have a will to do certain things, God will find a way to help you. I sent a nice letter of thanks to the Manager of the Hyatt in New Orleans.

Finally, I would like to give some advice as to what needs to be done to take Islam and Muslims out of the closet. The first thing we need to do is identify ourselves as Muslim wherever we have to register or show up in a meeting. Usually when some of these organizations want me to write down the name of the organization I am supposed to represent, instead of writing the name of my mosque or organization, I write down Islam. We don't have to look ethnic Muslim or dress like ethnic Muslims, but I have seen many non-ethnic Muslims look and dress like ethic Muslims. An example would be Iman Siraj Wahhaj and Yusuf Islam. We compliment our sisters for wearing the head cover and being identified as Muslim which is very nice and courageous of them. However, the Muslim young men who do not have a beard may have difficulty in being identified as Muslims. We should leave no opportunity to request a privilege which should be the right of Muslims such as a Muslim meal during airplane travel or interfaith conferences. Many times I have mentioned even to professional society and hospital meetings that I would like to make sure that no pork or alcohol is served at the conference.

The second thing we need to do is interact with non-Muslim organizations and groups of our concerns. For example, there are many anti-abortion groups, groups against homosexuality and pornography and drunken driving and so on. Muslims should be represented in each group. There are human rights organizations such as Amnesty and they have local chapters. Muslims should become part of these local chapters so that they can contribute both to the preservation of human rights and in all walks of violation of human rights and also be identified as Muslims. If there are any letters published in newspapers, again, any area of concern for the general public, we should write a letter in support expressing Islamic perspective on these issues and to let no opportunity go by to identify ourselves as Muslims individually or collectively. Recently some Muslim children in our area organized a trip to the bowling alley. They went in a group and they started bowling. Each time they would roll a ball, they would say "*Allahu akbar*" and finally, people around them started noticing that these were Muslims and that was why they were winning. Muslims in prisons, if they ask for their rights; for example, permissible food or right to perform the prescribed fast during Ramadan or to perform the Friday congregational prescribed prayer, they might be denied, but once they organize themselves and start asking these questions, they are given these privileges. Muslim parents should serve on school boards and review the books that are being taught to our children.

Many of the State Assembly and also the Congress have started their session with a prayer from a Muslim leader so more and more non-Muslims are noticing the presence of Muslims. We have to show them what Islam and Muslims are about with the example of our behavior and character in taking care of human needs.

I want to end this article with a light story. One Muslim woman in the modest charge, while looking for date in Ramadan in a supermarket to open her fast, asked the young boy, "Do you have date," and he replied, "I am not available tonight."

7 WHY ISLAM: ISLAM VS. SECULAR HUMANISM

INTRODUCTION

G ood, positive moral values are common to all religions and even a non-religious society and negative moral values are not appreciated by any religion or society.

While living in a non-Muslim society for more than two decades, I have met and known many non-Muslims who are good human beings and have many good qualities and good moral values. These non-Muslims have been my colleagues, co-workers, patients, neighbors and friends. I appreciate their honesty, integrity, truthfulness, and hard work. I wish some times they would become a Muslim, since Islam is the chosen religion of God.

However, when we Muslims look upon ourselves, we find some of us having very few qualities of being a Muslim or even of a human being. If this was not the case, then all negative moral values (for example, theft, murder, rape, adultery, dishonesty, bribery, injustice, slandering, backbiting, etc.) would have been non-existent in Muslim countries. But they do exist. If the believer (Muslim) actually believed in what he says he believes in, then what prevented him in practicing what he says he believes in. *"It is a grievous matter in the sight of God that you say that you do not do"* (61:3). *"Will you enjoin what is right on others and forget yourself"* (2:44).

UNIVERSAL MORAL VALUES

It is in human nature from birth to start recognizing certain behavior as good and normal and others as bad and abnormal. Influence of parents, peers, and society in general or state laws at large do modify, but appreciation of good qualities and denunciation of bad qualities are inborn parts of human nature. In fact, discarding the latter is a precursor of incorporation of former. You always take off soiled socks first before you put on new ones. Therefore, all religions and societies, whether they believe in God or not, to some degree still forbid and disapprove negative values (for example, selfishness, stealing, adultery, rudeness, misbehavior, falsehood, injustice, dishonesty, cruelty to fellow human beings and animals, fraud, bribery, slandering, backbiting, bigotry, breach of trust, rape, murder, robbery, etc.) Whether they are completely eliminated from society or not, at least these values are denounced by public in general or by the State. So Islam is not unique in forbidding the above, the only difference being that Islam does it more forcefully and offers more severe punishments for the offenders, both in the life here and in life hereafter.

In the same context, Islam, other religions, and even non-religious cultures appreciate positive moral values as a good quality in a human being. Therefore, kindness (to fellow human beings and animals), helping (the sick, the old, the neighbors), compassion, courage, patience, truthfulness, dignity, restraint, politeness, fidelity, justice, honesty, trust, loyalty and peace loving are all good qualities recognized by Islam and other moral systems.

So what are the differences? Why should a Muslim say that his moral values are better than that of others? The differences are on the following points:

1. The emphasis placed by Islam on good virtues is unparalleled and unsurpassed. The Quran and Hadith (traditions of Messenger Muhammad are full of instructions to Muslims on moral conduct in our day-to-day life. It is unfortunate that we Muslims are either not aware of orders of God or do not believe in them. To refresh the memory of those who might have forgotten, I am narrating a few examples.

GREETING

"Whenever you are welcomed with a greeting, then answer back with something better than it (or at least return it)" (4:36). A Tradition states, " Muslims owe to fellow Muslims six good points: 1) They should greet them when they see each other. 2) They should accept (invitation) when they are invited. 3) They should bless them when they sneezes. 4) They should visit each other when one is sick. 5) They should join in their funeral when they die. 6) They should desire for others what they desire for themselves" (see Bukhari and Muslim).

ANGER

"Restrain anger and pardon all men for God loves those who do good" (3:134).

ARROGANCE

"And walk not on earth haughtily (for) of a certainty you cannot rend the earth nor reach the mountain in height" (18:37). "And swell not the cheek with pride at people—for God loves not any arrogant boaster" (31:18).

RIDICULE

"O you who believe! Let not some men among you laugh at others; it may be that the latter are better than the former, or let not some women laugh at others; it may be the latter are better than the former, or defame, nor be sarcastic to each other, nor call each other by offensive nick-names" (49:11).

BACKBITING

"And spy not, neither backbite one another. Would one of you love to eat the flesh of his dead brother, No, you would hate it, and fear God, surely God is relenting, merciful" (49:12).

VAIN TALK

"When you hear vain talk, turn away from there and say, to us our deed and to you yours" (28:55). Tradition: "It is better to sit alone, than with bad people, it is still better to sit with good, than alone. It is better to

speak to a seeker of knowledge than to remain silent, but silence is better than idle words."

KEEPING ONE'S WORD

"Do not use God as an excuse in your oaths to keep yourself from being virtuous, doing your duty, and improving matters among mankind. God is alert and aware" (2:224).

GOSSIP AND RUMOR

"You who believe, if a scoundrel should bring you some piece of news, clear up the fact, lest you hurt some folk out of ignorance, and afterwards, feel regretful over what you have done" (49:6). Tradition: "Do not think evil of each other nor probe into each other's affair, nor excite one against the other. Keep yourself away from mutual hatred and jealousy." Tradition "One's friendship and enmity should be for the pleasure of God only. Whatever you give should be given because God likes it to be given and whatever you withhold should be withheld because God likes it not as a gift."

DUTIES TOWARDS NEIGHBORS

"Show kindness to both parents, to near relatives, orphans, the needy, the neighbor who is related as well as the neighbor who is a stranger, and your companion by your side and the wayfarer and anyone under your control" (4:36). Tradition on duty toward neighbors: The Messenger said,

1) The rights of neighbor were so much emphasized to him by Angel Gabriel that he feared neighbors may be asked to share inheritance.

2) A person who enjoys a full meal while his neighbor is starving has no faith in Islam.

3) A woman used to offer her prescribed prayers regularly, kept the prescribed fast and gave alms, but her neighbors were sick of her abusive tongue. The Messenger said that she deserved only hellfire.

4) Do not tease your neighbor by the smell of your delicious food. Rather, send a portion of it to him. If you bring fruits in your house, then send some to your neighbor, or at least do not throw the peels outside the door so so that your neighbors' children may not have a feeling of deprivation.

In brief, a practicing good Muslim is the one who submits to the Will of God, does good, and witnesses no falsehood, is a mirror for other Muslims, a leader among the believers, and cooperates with others in acts of virtue and piety and not in acts of sin and injustice.

After discussing common positive and negative moral behavior and values and elaborating the glorious injunctions of God and His Messenger for a Muslim's moral conduct, I want to establish the difference in the imposition and acceptance of Islamic versus non-Islamic laws of morality.

THE LAW MAKER

In non-Muslim societies, and even in atheistic civilization, there are moral laws. These laws are made by people for the benefit of people. "The Government of the People, by the People, and for the People," does not define what kind of people it is talking about. They may be God-fearing, good Christians or a group of mafia who may elect a leader of their choice or make a rule for themselves and call it a Democratic government. In Islam, the head of the state is God, He is the ultimate Law Maker. The Islamic government is the Government of God, by the people who believe in God, and for the pleasure of God..

THE ACCOUNTABILITY

A non-Muslim is responsible for his acts to the law makers and law-enforcing agencies of the state (the police, the FBI, the IRS). He may also have individual sense of responsibility to his self, family, employers, etc. Some criminals become habitual since they believe it is all right to do as long as you are not caught. The high rate of crime in this country (one murder every 27 minutes, one theft every 5 minutes, one motor vehicle stolen every 33 seconds, one robbery every 78 seconds, an assault every minute, one rape every 8 minutes, one burglary every 10 minutes) is because these criminals, while escaping the eyes of the police, FBI, etc. do not believe that someone else is watching them all the time and will take their account. True, these crimes exist even in Muslim countries but the incidence has no comparison. A Muslim is not only responsible to the laws of the land, but to the ultimate Law Maker, God He can escape the eyes of police, FBI and IRS but he will be caught on the Day of Judgment. The fear of God or Taqwa is what will prevent a Muslim from committing a crime.

THE ACCEPTANCE OF LAW

The State laws are imposed from the top (for example, the highest level of government upon the people) whether they like it or not. Therefore, the laws are made with some resistance since someone else (another human being) is deciding what is right for them or how they should behave. In Islam, the believer accepts the law himself, which is not imposed upon him. The compliance is great when one accepts the law from within rather than by force.

FLEXIBILITY IN LAW AND PUNISHMENT

Laws made by human beings are made according to the needs of human beings in that area and their cultural values. They vary in time and space. That is to say, what was unacceptable moral behavior (for example, degree of nudity 100 years ago) is perfectly acceptable now and what is normal in California (homosexuality) is unacceptable in a conservative state like Indiana.

However, Islamic moral laws remain unchanged for the last 1400 years. People have tried changing, but it has not helped them. In all means of modernization, by changing their dress, and script of writing, the "sick man of Europe" (Turkey) has remained a bankrupt, poor nation in political turmoil, much worse than she was "backward" under the Ottoman Empire. The modern Western laws are meant to crush the weak and protect the strong. The son of a rich man, after shooting the President, can hire an expensive lawyer and psychiatrist and get away by claiming temporary insanity while more than 1,000 not-so-rich fellow Americans convicted of similar or lesser crimes are waiting on the death row. In Islam, that is not the case, the law applies to everyone. The Messenger once said, "By God, even if my daughter Fatima is caught stealing, the same punishment will apply to her (cutting off the hand)."

THE CONCEPT OF CONFESSION AND REPENTANCE

In non-Islamic code of morality, the concept of repentance is different. The confession to the priest is not the same as repentance. The priest, a human being, should have no right to forgive the crimes which he will not be taken to account for on the Day of Judgment. After making confession, people do not correct but since their past sins are "forgiven," they get the green light to start over again and do the same thing. In Islam, since God is the Law Maker, it is He who can forgive and it is He to whom we can show our repentance. The doors of repentance are open. God says according to a Sacred Tradition, "O Son of Adam, as long as you call upon Me and ask of Me, I shall forgive you for what you have done and I shall not mind. O Son of Adam, were your sins to reach the clouds of sky and were you then to ask forgiveness of Me, I would forgive you. O Son of Adam, were you to come to Me with sins nearly as great as the earth, and were you then to face Me, ascribing no partners to Me, I would bring you forgiveness nearly as great as it." And in Quran, God says, *"And as far as those who believe and do good, we shall remit them from their evil deed and shall repay them the best for what they did"* (29:7.)

Finally, a summary of the Ten Commandments of the Islamic moral code are given beautifully in 6:151-153:

1. *Do not associate anything with Him (God).*

2. *Show kindness toward both (your) parents.*

3. *Do not kill your children because of poverty. We shall provide for you as well as for them.*

4. *Do not indulge in shameful acts, be they open or secret.*

5. *Do not kill any person whom God has forbidden except through (due process of) law. He has instructed in this so that you may reason.*

6. *Do not approach an orphan's wealth before he comes of age except to improve it.*

7. *Give full measures and weight in all fairness. We do not assign any one more than he can cope with.*

8. *Whenever you speak, be just even though it concerns a close relative.*

9. *Fulfill God's Covenant. Thus He has instructed you so that you may bear it in mind.*

10. *This is My straight road, so follow it and do not follow other paths which will separate you from His path. Thus He has instructed you so that you may do your duty.*

And for the Christians and Jews who might be reading this article, I repeat the call of God: *"Say, O people of the scripture! Come to an agreement between us and you, that we shall worship none but God, and that we shall ascribe no partners unto Him, and none of us shall take others for lords beside God. And if they turn away, then say: "Bear witness that we are they who have surrendered (unto Him)"* (3:64).

PART V:
ISLAMIC BELIEFS

*"Say: We believe in God and what has been sent down to us,
and what was sent down to Abraham, Ishmael, Isaac, Jacob
and their descendants,
and what was given to Moses, Jesus
and the prophets by their Lord.
We do not discriminate against any one of them
and are committed to (live at) peace with Him" (3:84).*

1 PEACE THROUGH SUBMISSION

Religion as understood by others is "a way of worship of (a) God." This philosophy requires the presence of (a) God. The religion in Islam is not a way of worship, but a way of life (in a most natural way). So anyone (or anything) which submits (or follows) the natural ways is a Muslim. This includes human beings, animal, plants, planets, stars, etc. This is the only way they can stay in peace. A planet orbits on an appointed route. A tree grows in a particular direction. If this pattern is disturbed (going against the will of God) there will be no peace. So a Muslim is the one who attains peace within and without by submitting his will to the will of God.

God says in the Quran, "*If any one desires a religion other than submission the the will of God (islam) it will be accepted and in the hereafter he will be in the ranks of those who are losers*" (3:85). "*Moreover He comprehended in HIs design the sky and it had been (as) smoke. He said to it and to the earth, 'Come you together willingly or unwillingly' and they said, 'We do come together in willing obedience'*" (41:11). "'*O you who believe, accept Islam whole-heartedly and do not follow the footsteps of the devil for he is your open enemy*" (2:208). "*Those who do not believe and die as non-believers, on them is the curse of God and of angels and of men combined*" (2:161). "*Those who become disbelievers after becoming believers, God will not forgive them*" (3:90). "*O you who believe, if you follow the People of the Book they will make you disbelievers after you have believed*" (3:100).

So far we have discussed the need for the submission to the Will of

God. Now we would like to know how we do it. This is rather simple in the sense that the Will of God as described in the Quran is not against the laws of nature. So if we follow the laws of nature and do not over ride it with the laws of human beings (as developed by his/her desires and imagination), then we are doing it find. Let us examine the will of God and submission to it as described in the Quran. On this earth we have been given a contract with God to carry out His orders in an appointed time. If we do well in our part of the contract, He will keep His part of the contract. What is the contract?

God says in the Quran, "*I am with you: if you establish regular prayer, practice regular charity, believe in My Messengers, honor and assist them, and loan to God a beautiful loan (charity). Of course I will wipe out from you your sins and admit you to heaven with rivers flowing beneath but if any of you, after this, resists the faith, he has truly wandered from the simple path*" (5:13). "*It is not righteousness that you turn your faces towards the East or the West but the righteousness is to believe in God, the Last Day and the angels and the Book and the Messengers; to spend of your substance out of love for Him, for your relatives, for orphans, for the traveler, for those who ask, ask for the ransom of slaves; to be steadfast in prayer, practice regular charity, to fulfill the contract which you have made*" (2:177).

God requires that we submit our will to His Will. "*Your God is one God, submit then your will to Him and give good news to those who humble themselves*" (22:34). "*Who can be better in religion than he who submits his whole self (physical and spiritual) to God, does good and follows the ways of Abraham for God did take Abraham for a friend*" (4:125).

From here onward we will examine what comes in our way or what prevents us from submission to the Will of God. It is the attractions of this life, our temptations, vain desires. Let us examine what the Quran says about the life of this world. "*What is the life of this world but play and amusement? But best is the home in the Hereafter for those who are righteous. Will you not then understand*" (6:32). "*The life of this world is attractive to those who reject faith and they scoff at those who believe. But the righteous will be above them on the Day of Judgment for God bestows His abundance without measure on whom He will*" (2:212). "*Leave alone those who take their way of life to be mere play and amusement and are deceived by the life of this world. But proclaim (to them) this (truth): That every soul delivers itself to ruin by its own acts. It will find for itself no protector or intercessor except God. If it offered every ransom, none will be accepted. Such is (the end of) those who cause themselves to ruin by their own acts. They will have to drink boiling water and for punishment, one most grievous for they persisted in rejecting God*" (6:70). "*Such as took their way of life to be mere amusement and play and were deceived by the life of this world, that day shall we forget them as they forgot the meeting of this day of theirs and as they were bent upon rejecting our Signs*" (7:51). "*Did you then think that We created you for mere idle play and that you would not have to return to us?*" (23:115).

So if the life of this not for play and attractions or possessions of this world are of not much value, then what is of value? "*Beautiful for mankind is the love of the joys (that come) from women, and offspring, and stored up heaps of gold and silver and horses, cattle and land. That is comfort of the life of the world. But nearness to God is the best of the goals (to return to)*" (3:14).

However, we human beings do not always appreciate what God selects for us. "*Fighting (in the way of God) is prescribed for you and you dislike it. But it is possible that you dislike a thing which is good for you and that you love a thing which is bad for you but God knows and you know not*" (2:216). "*Say not equal are things that are bad and things that are good even though the abundance of the bad may dazzle you. So fear God oh you that understand that you may prosper*" (5:103).

The second thing which prevents human beings from bowing down to the Will of God is his arrogance (*takabbar*) and self-conceit (*kibr*). This is the root of spiritual darkness and roots in the fact of the human being's concept of self-assurance and over-confidence in himself, his powers and imagination. This is the cause of rebellion in him.

The Quran reminds him/her of his/her humble origin. "*Has not the human being seen that we have created him from a drop of fluid yet lo he is an open opponent*" (36:77). "*He has created the heaven and the earth with Truth. Far is He above the partners they associate with Him. He has created the human being from a drop of fluid yet behold! he becomes an open disputer!*" (16:3).

After rejection of faith (*kufr*) and association of partners to God (*shirk*), the arrogance (*kibr*) is the third most deadly sin. Iblis was not guilty of being an unbeliever (in God) or of ascribing partners to Him, but of arrogance for which he was thrown out. "*And behold, we said to the angels, bow down to Adam and they bowed down; not so Iblis. He refused* and was arrogant. He was those who reject faith" (2:34). "God said: What prevented you (Iblis) from bowing down when I commanded you? He (Iblis) said: I am better than he (man); You created me from fire and him from clay. God said: Get down from this. It is not for you to be arrogant here. Get out for you are the meanest (of creatures)" (7:12-13). Refusal, rejection (of truth) and heedlessness are part of arrogance and the opposite of submission and lead to rebellion and make Iblis satanic. When the unbeliever makes Iblis as his guide that person takes up the qualities of his guide, too.

The Quran mentions arrogance in many places: *"When it is said to them (unbelievers), prostrate, they do not"* (77:48). *"And when the Quran is read to them, they fall not prostrate on the contrary, they reject it"* (84:21-22). *"But those who reject our Signs and treat them with arrogance, they are the companions of the fire to dwell therein forever"* (7:36). *"To those who reject our Signs and treat them with arrogance, no opening will there be of the gates of heaven nor will they enter into the garden until the camel can pass through the eye of a needle. Such is Our reward for those who do wrong"* (7:40). *"Your God is God. As to those who believe not in the Hereafter, their heart refuses to know and they are arrogant. Undoubtedly God knows what they conceal and what they reveal. Surely He loves not the arrogant"* (16:22-23).

In conclusion, God punishes those who fail to submit because of their arrogance. He is pleased and protects those who accept faith as mentioned in the Quran in the following places: *"God is the protector of those who have faith. From the depth of darkness He will lead them forward into light. Those who reject faith and appoint evil ones as their guide, they will lead them into darkness from light. They will be the residents of hell to live there forever"* (2:257). *"God wishes to turn to you but wishes of those who follow their bad desires is that you should turn away from Him far, far away. God wishes to lighten your difficulties for the human being was created weak"* (4:27-28). *"Oh you who believe, if you fear God, He will grant you a criterion (to judge between right and wrong), remove from you (all) evil (that may afflict you) and forgive you for God is the Lord of grace unbound"* (8:29).

2 PRACTICING PIETY

Talking about piety (*taqwa*) or writing about it is easy. It is the practice of piety that is most difficult, especially trying to practice it 24 hours a day, 7 days a week. Islam is not a weekend religion, but demands that we are Muslim all of the time. "*O you who believe, accept Islam wholeheartedly, and do not follow the footsteps of the devil, for he is your open enemy*" (2:208).

It is not easy to translate or describe the meaning of the word piety. In the Quran it is mentioned in various ways to mean: being God-conscious; being God fearing; to be pious; being careful or heeding God's call; and having self restraint along Islamic lines.

Now let us review some of the verses of the Quran describing piety. The first usage is in the beginning of Surah al-Baqarah. "*This is the book, in it is guidance for sure (without doubt) for those who practice piety (muttaqin)*" (2:2). In the following verses (3-4) the features of a pious person are described as those who believe in the unseen, establish regular prayer, spend from what God has given them, who believe in the Quran and the holy scriptures that came before the Quran, and those who believe in the hereafter. In the fifth verse their reward for being pious is described as, "*They are on (true) guidance from their Lord, and it is these who will prosper.*"

PIETY DESCRIBED AS A PROTECTIVE SHIELD

"*O you children of Adam. We have given dress to you to cover your*

185

shame, as well as to be an adornment to you but the dress of righteous-
ness) (piety, taqwa) is the best. Such are the signs of God that you may
receive admonition" (7:26) And, *"O you who believe, save yourself and*
your families from a fire whose fuel is men and stones, over which are
angels stern and severe, who fail not (from executing) the commands they
receive from Allah, but do precisely what they are ordered" (66:6).

PIETY DESCRIBED AS GOD-AWARENESS

"O mankind, be conscious of your duty to God, who created you from
a single person, created of like nature his mate, and from twain scattered
countless men and women. Be conscious of God, through whom you
demand your mutual rights and wombs (that bore you). For God ever
watches over you" (4:1). God awareness is described as knowing that
God is watching over you. Caliph Umar has said, "It is as if you are going
on a path with a lot of bushes and you fold your clothes to avoid thorns
setting into them."

PIETY DESCRIBED AS A TOOL TO LEARN DISCIPLINE (SELF-RESTRAINT)

"O you who believe' Fasting is prescribed for you as it was pre-
scribed for those before you, that you may learn self restraint" (2:183).

PIETY DESCRIBED AS AN ACT OF PIETY AND RIGHTEOUSNESS

"But those who receive guidance, He increases the light of guidance
and bestows on them their piety and restraint from evil" (47:17). *"But*
none will keep it in the remembrance except as God wills; He is the Lord
of Righteousness, and the Lord of Forgiveness" (74:56). *"The most hon-*
ored of you in the sight of God is he who is the most righteous of you, and
God has full knowledge and is acquainted will all things" (49:13).

PIETY DESCRIBED AS BEING GOD-FEARING

"O you who believe, fear God as He should be feared, and die not
except in a state of Islam" (3:102). *"O you who believe, fear God and let*
every soul look to what provision He has sent forth for the morrow.
Yea,fear God, for God is well acquainted with all that you do" (59:18).

The fear of God is different than for example the fear of a lion, from whom we expect no mercy. We fear God for His displeasure, losing His blessings, and incurring punishment. We fear Him with love, not hate. "*And those who fear the displeasure of their Lord*" (70:27). "*But believers are most fervent in their love of God*" (2:165).

REWARDS FOR BEING PIOUS

The Quran mentions many rewards for the pious. "*Nay, those who keep their promise and practice righteousness, verily God loves those who are pious (practice righteousness)*" (3:76). "*O you who believe. If you fear God, He will grant you a criterion (to judge between right and wrong), remove from you all evil that may affect you, and forgive you for God is the Lord of Grace unbound*" (8:29). "*Those who fear and act righteously, on them shall be no fear nor shall they grieve*" (7:35). "*Say, if you do love God, then follow me (Muhammad). God will love you and forgive you your sins. For God is oft-forgiving, Merciful*" (3:31).

In summary, piety is being conscious of God, to seek manners of pleasing Him, and avoiding His displeasure, in order to receive His love, guidance, and forgiveness and to protect ourselves from hellfire. We can only practice piety (awareness of God if we can recognize Him through His signs. For a detailed documentation of His signs, see 30:20-60. The signs described are in the creation of our body, nature, the universe, life and death, the operation of this earth, and the signs the Prophets brought with them.

HOW TO INCREASE PIETY

After recognizing God, and establishing the belief of Him in our heart, we can attempt to increase His awareness (with His permission) by doing the following:

1. Acts of Worship: The prescribed prayers, the prescribed fast, the pilgrimage, and the poor-due. In addition to five daily prescribed prayers, the prayer between midnight to the time of the dawn prescribed prayer (*tahajjud*) is highly recommended and mentioned in the Quran (17:79). In addition to reciting the Quran during the prescribed prayer, further recitation is good, especially in the early hours of the morning.

2. Acts Of Asking For Forgiveness: "*Then Adam learned words of forgiveness, from his Lord and his Lord turned towards him, for He is oft-*

forgiving, Most Merciful" (2:37). Those words of forgiveness taught to Adam and Eve were: They said *"Our Lord, we have wronged our souls. If you forgive us not, and bestow not upon us your mercy, we shall certainly be lost"* (7:23).

Forgiveness is the reward of repentance which comes out of piety. *"He is the one who accepts repentance from His servants and forgives sins and He knows all that you do. And He listens to those who believe and do acts of righteousness, and gives them increase of His bounty"* (42:25-26).

3. Acts of Communication With God (remembrance, *dhikr*): We should communicate with God all the time, no matter in what state we are and whatever we are doing. *"And your Lord says call on Me and I will answer your calls"* (40:60). *"When my servants ask you concerning Me, I am indeed close to them: I listen to the prayers of every supplicant when he calls upon Me. Let them also with a will listen to My call, and believe in Me, that they may walk in the right way"* (2:186). *"Those who believe, and whose hearts find rest in the remembrance of God, for without doubt in the remembrance of God do hearts find rest"* (13:28).

Among the recommended daily practices to increase depth of faith and awareness of God are keeping ablution intact; performing the prescribed prayer on time; recitation of the Quran; remembrance of God in one's spare time; and remembering death as it can get us at any time, anywhere. Also, staying in the company of pious Muslims who do all these to help strengthen their faith. I ask God to forgive my mistakes and give me His Awareness and His Pleasure as a result, Amin.

3 LOVE AND UNITY IN THE CAUSE OF GOD

G od says in the Quran, "*O you who believe, observe your duty to God with right observance, and die not except in a state of submission (to Him). And hold fast, all of you together, to the rope of God, and do not separate, and remember God's favor unto you: how you were enemies and He put love between your hearts so that you became as brothers by His grace: and how you were upon the brink of a fire and He saved you from it. Thus God makes clear His revelations unto you so that you may be guided*" (3:102-103).

In the above verses belief, piety, Islam (submission to God) are tied together and there is an order to hold on to them. If we do so, then God grants us love and brotherhood and saves us from the fire. It is the same love which God has mentioned in Surah al-Infal. "*And as for the believers, God has joined their hearts with love for you spent all that is in the earth, you could not have done it, but God has done it. He is Mighty and Wise*" (8:63).

The Islamic ties of brotherhood has been mentioned in several places *in Quran, but to quote one in Surah al-Hujurat, "The believers are nothing else other than brothers, Thus make peace between your brethren and observe your duty to God that you may haply receive His mercy*" (49:10).

Love and brotherhood among Muslims has often been emphasized by the Prophet Muhammad (ﷺ) in many places:

1. "None of you will enter paradise until you have faith, and you will not complete your faith until you love one another" (Bukhari).

2. "On the day of Judgment, when there will be no shade except the

shade of God, one of the six categories of Muslims who will be under the shade are the ones who loved other Muslims just for the pleasure of God" (Muslim).

3. Some Companions came to the Prophet (ﷺ) and asked, "O Prophet (ﷺ), we do all the rituals, but we do not feel the sweetness of faith in our hearts. Tell us some remedy." The Prophet (ﷺ) said, "There are three things you can do to increase the sweetness of faith in your heart: a) love other Muslims just for the sake of God; b) love God and His Messenger more than anything else; and c) hate to go back to rejection of faith" (Bukhari and Muslim).

However, in spite of such clear injunctions to us about love, unity and brotherhood, we see ourselves being disunited, disliking, and even fighting on all levels, individually, sectarian, tribal, and even one country against another, why?

The main reasons for disunity are:

1) False pride in our ethnic and linguistic origin. The creation of mankind into tribes and speaking different languages was in the design of God. "*O mankind, We created you from a single pair of a male and a female and made you unto nations and tribes, SO THAT YOU MAY KNOW EACH OTHER (not that you may despise each other). The most honored of you in the light of God is the most righteous of you, and God has full knowledge and He is Aware*" (49:13). "*And among His signs are the creation of the heaven and earth, and the variation in your language and your colors; verily in that are signs for those who know*" (30:22).

Thus it should be clear that our natural differences (race, color, language) are from God, and do not justify hating each other. Piety is the only criterion for superiority. In the same context, it is not necessary to mix all tribes into one. Let them enjoy their ethnic food, dress, and language as long as Islamic principles are not broken. Nationalism is when one puts his love before the orders of God and His Messenger. In other words, in his love of his nation is he willing to disobey God?

2) The second reason for our disunity is the lack of consultation and miscommunication. The concept of consultation has been emphasized in the Quran in family life. For example, "*If they (the parents) both decide on weaning by mutual consultation*" (2:233), in disputes and "*consult them*" (3:157).

Thus we see that Prophet Muhammad (ﷺ) always consulted with his companions at the time of war and in the affairs of Madinah. In fact, during the battle of Badr, he changed the position of the troops on the advice of an ordinary soldier. The four guided caliphs (Abu Baker, Umar, Uthman, and Ali, may God be pleased with them) during their rule always consulted with each other in complicated matters.

However, in present-day organizations as well as Muslim governments the process of consultation is forgotten. One person decides what he is doing is best for the organization or country. This generates a lack of trust and cooperation from the masses.

3) The third reason is a lack of love. The virtues of love as mentioned in the Quran and Traditions are cited at the beginning of this article. We forget, however, that hate and animosity is a work of Satan. *"Satan seeks only to cast among you enmity and hate"*(5:91). Satan does so by making us backbite, spy on one another, defame, call offensive nicknames, gossip, ridicule, etc., all of which we are told to avoid in the Quran (Surah al-Hujurat).

Differences of opinion are justified, and are not a valid reason for permanent animosity. For example soon after Abu Bakr became caliph, a new group of converts refused to pay *zakat*, saying that it was due only when the Prophet (ص) was alive. Umar initially sided with them, citing a Tradition that belief in God and the Messenger was enough for salvation. The caliph Abu Bakr disagreed, saying that prescribed prayer and prescribed poor-due are tied together in the Quran and are a part of faith. Umar then realized his mistake.

In another example, at the siege of Jerusalem by Abu Ubayda, the Christians refused to surrender until they met the caliph. The message went to Madinah and consultation was held. Uthman disagreed, saying the city was under siege and that it was only a matter of time. Ali agreed that the caliph Umar should go and meet them and Umar took Ali's advice.

HOW TO INCREASE LOVE AND UNITY

1. Know your duty toward your fellow Muslim. "A Muslim is a Muslim's brother. He does not wrong him. If anyone cares for his brother's needs, God will care for his needs. If anyone will remove his brother's anxiety, God will remove his anxiety on the Day of Judgment and if any conceals a Muslim's secret, God will conceal his secrets on the Day of Judgment" (Bukhari).

In our personal dealings, we should remember God's order as mentioned in Surah al-Hujurat.

2. Be gentle in criticism with Muslims and tough with unbelievers. *"They are hard on disbelievers but merciful to each other"* (Quran). Presently, however, we see the opposite. We seem to love non-Muslims more than fellow Muslims.

3. Protect each other. *"Believers, men and women, are protectors of one another"* (9:71). During the reign of caliph Umar, he received the news that one Jewish tailor sewed a dress for a Muslim woman that he designed intentionally to fall apart in the bazaar so as to humiliate her and disgrace the Muslim community. This was enough for the caliph to threaten war on the entire tribe. He did not ask whether the woman was a good Muslim or a bad one, whether she prayed five times a day and paid the poor-due, etc. But these days we find a reason not to support a Muslim in his difficult days by putting all kinds of labels on his faith and practices. Finally, whatever we do, we should do it with the belief that we are doing it for the sake of God. *"Say: My prayer, my sacrifice, my life and my death are for God, the Lord of the Worlds"* (6:16).

4 WHO CONTROLS OUR DESTINY?

In spite of prohibition from God and also from the Messenger refraining people from indulging in futile discussions of the destiny of the human being, this subject comes up in discussion anyway. *"Oh you who believe! Ask not questions about things which if made plain to you may cause you trouble. But if you ask about things when the Quran is being revealed, they will be made plain to you, God will forgive those for God is oft forgiving most forbearing"* (5:104).

NATURE OF ARGUMENTS

The questions that are most asked concerning our after life are:

1. Are we free agents? Do we control our destiny or are we just following a pre-decreed path?

2. If we are free to make our destiny, where does God fit in?

3. If God has full knowledge of our deeds and controls our destiny, why are we held responsible for our actions?

4. If God did not guide us to be good, why does He punish us when we are bad?

NON-MUSLIM VIEW OF PRE-DESTINY

Philosophers in general have some vague concepts. One group believes that God has knowledge of our actions but only after the act is committed. Others who are not seriously committed to belief (of God) believe in luck or time controlling their destiny. A third group regards men as totally independent.

MUSLIM VIEW OF PRE-DESTINY

The term used in Quran is "*al-qadar*." The translation of *qadar* is not pre-destiny but "due proportions" or due measures. God has created everything in due proportions. "*It is He who created all things and ordered them in due proportions*" *(taqdira)*. (25:2). "*And the command of God is a decree determined*" *(maqdura)*" (33:38).

AREAS OF OUR CONTROL/LACK OF CONTROL

There are two types of control in the physiology of our body:

a) Central nervous system control, when our body movements and reflex actions are controlled by our mind through nerves connecting the muscles attached to joints.

b) Autonomic nervous system or involuntary system, in which the mind has little control on heart rate, body temperature, blood pressure, etc. They are controlled by hormones, whose secretions depend on the need.

Similarly, in our actions, there are two areas of control:

a) We have no control, for example, on our skin color, facial features, sex, etc., and there will be no questions asked about them from us on the Day of Judgment.

b) We do have control over simple decisions in our life, i.e., to believe in God or not to believe in Him, to give a known poison to a sick person versus to give him a known medicine, to spend money on gambling or on charity. We can make such decisions if we have clear belief in the advantages versus disadvantages of such action.

OUR CRITERIA OF GOOD VERSUS EVIL

Human beings cannot always make the decision on what is good or not good for them, like a patient who cannot make the decision whether treatment is good for him or not. He has to rely on the knowledge and experience of his doctor. "*Fighting (in the way of God) is prescribed for you and you dislike it. But it is possible that you dislike a thing which is good for you and that you love a thing which is bad for you. But God knows and you know not*" (2:216). Example: Is rainfall good or bad? Rainfall is good for the farmer but is not so good for city dwellers where traffic is disrupted, is good for flowers and vegetable plants, but is bad for thorn bushes and weeds, is good for one living in a brick house who can enjoy it, but is bad for one living in a mud house. So the good becomes bad or vice versa depending on who receives or what purpose is achieved.

(b) I have to get to the airport to catch a plane. My wife gives me food late, I get a last minute phone call and then I get caught in a traffic jam. Well, I miss the plane, so I am upset with everyone who caused this. I have a negative view. Upon my return back to the house, I listen to the radio and hear that the plane I was to board, crashed in midair upon take-off. I thank God for saving my life. Bad becomes good. *"He cannot be questioned about his acts, but they (as human being) will be questioned (about theirs)"* (21:23).

OUR CONCEPT OF GOD'S GUIDANCE AND HIS METHODS OF GUIDANCE

God guides only those who believe in His guidance, asks for it, and then accept it for the purpose of acting upon it. Then not only He guides them, but increases their guidance, and gives them a criterion to judge between right and wrong so that they can make better decisions. To the contrary, those who reject Him as the guide, and are bent upon evil as directed by their vain desire, pride (in self), God removes His protection from them, lets them go astray, and seals their heart that nothing good enters it, seals their hearing that they can't hear good (i.e., good sounds bad to them) and puts a covering on their eyes so that they can't see right (eye does not see, what mind does not know, and the heart does not accept). To those who love God, God loves them, and takes special care of them in protecting them from evil future.

If you asked a policeman for road directions, if he knew you and loved you (as a friend), he would not only give the right direction but most likely would say "I don't want you to be wandering. I will take you there myself." On the other hand, if you were arrogant and disbelieving, the policeman has no more responsibility other than just pointing to the direction to which you should be going. This is the difference of guidance of God to believer versus general humanity.

Let us examine some verses of Quran about guidance: *"God is the protector of those who have faith; from the depth of darkness, He will lead them forth into the light. Of course, those who reject faith, the patrons are the evil ones; from light they will lead them forth into the depth of darkness. They will be companions of fire, to dwell therein (forever)* (2:257). *"O You who believe! If you fear God, He will grant you a criterion (to judge between right and wrong), remove from you (all) evil (that may afflict) you, and forgive, for God is the Lord of Grace unbounded."* (8:29). *"Say: God's guidance is the (only) guidance and we have been directed to submit ourselves to the Lord of the Worlds"* (6:71).

MY QUESTION TO THE INTELLECTUAL

Is it not simple, easier, and preferable way to be guided by God in this dark area of destiny of future and present, than take upon ourselves to venture?

BELIEF IN PRE-DESTINY AFFECTING OUR DAY TO DAY LIFE

Muslims accept failures and calamities as a test and warning from their Creator., Therefore, they ask for God's forgiveness and His help. *"Be sure we shall test you with something of fear and hunger, small loss in goods or lives or the fruit (of your toil) but give glad tiding to those who patiently persevere who say when afflicted with calamity, 'To God we belong, and to Him is our return.'"*

Then for Muslims believing in the Will of God accept illness better and accept treatment as the Will of God and in anxiety, they do not panic nor do they have suicidal depression in failures and misfortunes because they know that God says in Quran, *"No misfortune can happen on earth or in your soul but is recorded in a decree before we bring it into existence, that is truly easy for God"* (57:22).

The answers to the questions asked in the beginning are that (1) God has knowledge of our past, present and future, (2) He has knowledge of our will, intentions and power to change our destiny according to our intentions and efforts, and (3) the human being has limited free will which he can use to his advantage or to his detriment. *"And if your Lord willed, all who are in the earth would have believed. Would You (O Muhammad) compel men until they are believed? It is not for any to believe except by the permission of God. His wrath is upon those who have no common sense"* (10:99-100). *"Surely God does not change the condition in which a people are in until they change that which is in themselves"* (13:11).

Therefore, as Shaykh Jafar Idris puts it in his book *The Process of Islamization*, "The human being cannot do anything against the Will of God, but God has willed to give him the freedom to choose and power to realize some of his intentions even if they go against the guidance given by God. One of the important areas in which God gave man to act is his internal state. But since much of what happens to man depends upon what kind of internal state he has, faith can be said to be largely responsible for his destiny."*What ever good (O man) happens to you is from God; but whatever evil happens to you is from your (own) soul"* (4:79).

Those who are used to driving on icy roads in Midwest winters, can understand the following example. A man sets out from his house on an early winter morning to go to work. He finds the road very icy and hazardous for driving. Unless he takes special precautions, he is destined to end up in the hospital with an accident rather than his place of work. Since he cannot control the road conditions, he should try to control what he can, i.e., his speed and steering. Our actions are the only thing which controls our destiny which has already been predecided by God. Surah al-Asr. *"Verily man is in loss. Except such as have faith, and do righteous deeds and (join together) in the mutual teaching of truth, and of patience and constancy."*

5 Lying —A Disease of the Heart

L ying and falsehood are universal problems and a root of many other problems on an individual and public level, in spoken and written words, in the media and in politics, in business and personal dealings, by believers and non-believers alike, although the degree, magnitude and frequency may vary.

Lying is against human nature, against physiology, and like a disease, has its own signs and symptoms. The act of lying produces inner conflicts between various control centers of the brain. The moment one begins to lie, the body sends out contradictory signals to cause facial muscle twitching, expansion and contraction of pupils, perspiration, flushing of cheeks, increased eye blinking, tremor of hand and rapid heart rate. These constitute the basis of lie detector instruments. In addition, you will notice the liar is unconsciously doing some movements, like covering his mouth, nose touching, eye rubbing, scratching the side of the neck, rubbing his ear, etc. One of the most clear signs is that the liar keeps his palms closed and eyes pointed to another direction than facing the person eye to eye when he is lying. A liar is aware of his body signals, therefore he finds lying easier when no one can see him, i.e., on the phone or writing.

What is Lying?

Lying is opposite of the truth. So anything which is not truth for sure is a lie. A lie, therefore, could be something said or written, which could be totally or partially baseless, unreal, made-up, distorted or exaggerated, i.e., if a 5 foot pole is described as a 10 foot pole. Similarly giving praise out of proportion to someone is a form of lie.

WHAT ARE THE MOTIVES OF A LIAR?

A liar tells a lie for the purpose of: a) concealing the truth, since he is afraid of truth or punitive actions by law or individuals once the truth is established, b) for cheating and deceiving others and enjoying their misery like Satan did to Adam, and c) short-term worldly gains, i.e., gaining their favors or monetary gains until the lies are not exposed as a lie.

FORMS OF LYING

The worst lying form is lying upon the God and the Messenger, i.e., attributing things to God or the Prophet without it actually being the case, *"And if he had invented false saying concerning Us, We assuredly had taken him by the right hand and then severed his life artery"* (67:44-46). Concealing the witness is a form of lying. *"Hide not the testimony he who hides it, verily his heart is sinful. (2:283). God is aware of what you do."* Concealing the truth is a crime in itself. *"Confound not truth with falsehood, nor knowingly conceal the truth"* (2:42).

Hypocrites are liars, too, because they lie to themselves. *"In their heart, there is a disease and God increases their disease, a painful doom is theirs because they lie"*(2:10). *"God knows that you are His Messenger while God testifies that hypocrites are liars"* (63:1).

THE QURAN ABOUT LAIRS

"God guides not one who is a prodigal, a liar" (40:28). *"God guides not him who is a liar, an ingrate"* (39:3). *"God's curse will rest on him if he is a liar"* (24:7).

THE MESSENGER ABOUT LIARS

a. "Verily, truth leads to virtue and virtue leads to paradise and a true man continues to speak truth until he becomes the most truthful person. Lies lead to evil and evil leads to hell and a liar continues to lie till he is listed as a highest ranking liar before God" (Bukhari).

b. The use of tongue for lying, backbiting, speaking ill, etc. Yusuf ibn

Abdullah states that he asked Prophet Muhammad (ص), " O Messenger of God, what do you think most dreadful thing for me?" Yusuf said, the Messenger caught hold of his tongue and said "This." (Tirmidhi).

c. Bahz Ibn Hakim related that the Messenger said "Destruction is for the man who speaks lies for the amusement of other people. Destruction for him." (Tirmidhi).

d. Sufyan Ibn Usaid reported that the Messenger said "The biggest breach of trust is that you tell a thing to your brother who believes it to be true, whereas you have lied to him" (Abu Daud).

LYING EVER JUSTIFIED?

There are no absolute justifications in Islam and the Prophet has asked us to tell truth even under the harshest circumstances of oppression. However, one may choose not to tell the truth when:

a. He is under oppression and there is danger of losing his life if he told the truth. Shaykh Saadi narrates a story, "A cruel king ordered an innocent man present in his court to be killed because of his lack of manners. Hearing this, the villager started to curse the king in his native language. The king asked the prime minister, who understood that man's language, to tell him what that man was saying The wise minister, instead of telling the truth, told the king this man is sorry for his conduct, praising his greatness and asking for his mercy The king was affected and he spared the life of that innocent man." Shaykh Saadi calls this a "lie with wisdom."

b. To promote mutual relationship between spouse, i.e., if wife asks you, "Am I beautiful?" or "Do you love me?" there is nothing wrong with saying "Yes," even if this is not the case.

c. While making peace between two quarreling parties, instead of igniting them against each other, i.e., "He said such and such bad thing about you," just say,"He says such and such good thing about you." Tradition: He is not a liar who tries to bring peace between two people by trying to tell the truth only as described in Surah al-Anbiya (21:62).

d. To make unbelievers realize the truth (21:62-65) When Prophet Abraham broke all the idols except the biggest one, the unbelievers entered the temple. Abraham hid and put his ax in the hand of the chief idol. They asked, "Who broke our gods?" He said, "Ask the chief idol, he has the ax." They said, "Don't you know he can't speak or do anything?" Abraham said, "That's what I have been telling you, so worship

God, rather than these stones who cannot harm or profit you."

VIRTUES OF TELLING THE TRUTH

Truthfulness is a command of God, part of faith, and a quality of must for all prophets and is mentioned in 100 places in the Quran. To name a few:

"So God may reward the truthful for their truthfulness" (33:24). *"You who believe, heed God and stand by those who are truthful"* (9:119). *"You who believe, guard your duty to God, and speak words straight to the point"* (33:70). *"The steadfast and the truthful and the obedient and those who spend, those who pray for pardons in the watches of the night"* (3:17). *"Believers are merely the ones who believe in God and His Messenger. They never doubt, and strive for God's sake with their property and persons. Those are the Truthful"* (49:15).

It is not necessary for me to relate the Traditions about truthfulness since the life of Muhammad ibn Abdullah (ص) was nothing but truth. He was confirmed as a truthful person even before he became Prophet and during his prophethood, even his enemies confirmed that he was truthful as described by Abu Sufyan in the court of the emperor of Rome.

6 THE LAST SERMON OF PROPHET MUHAMMAD (ص): CONFIRMATION OF THE MAIN POINTS FROM THE QURAN

66 *Oh Prophet, We have sent you as a witness, news bearer and a warner and as someone who invites people to God by His permission and a shining Lamp*" (33:45-46). Prophet Muhammad (ص) who was sent to mankind as a news bearer and a warner for he spoke the truth and did not invent something of his own. The purpose of this article is to confirm the statements made by Prophet Muhammad (ص) during his farewell address during the last pilgrimage (10 AH). After praising and thanking God, the Messenger said, "Oh people, listen to my words carefully for I know not whether I will meet you on such an occasion again."

TRUST AND ACCOUNTABILITY

Sermon: "Oh people, just as you regard this month, this day, this city as sacred, so regard the life and property of every Muslim as a sacred trust. Remember that you will indeed appear before God and answer for your actions."

Quran: "*If anyone killed a person unless it is for a murder or spreading mischief on earth it would be as it he killed the whole mankind), and if anyone who saved a life, it would be as if he saved the life of whole mankind*" (5:32). "*Then on that day not a soul will be wronged in the least and you shall but be prepaid in the needs of your past deeds*" (36:54).

203

FINANCIAL OBLIGATIONS

Sermon: "Return the things kept with you as trust (*amanah*) to their rightful owners."

Quran: *"If one of you entrusts (something) the one who has been entrusted with it should hand over his security and he should heed God and not hide any testimony. Anyone who hides it—has a sinful heart"* (2:283).

INTEREST (RIBAH)

Sermon: "All dues of interest shall stand cancelled and you will have only your capital back. Allah has forbidden interest, and I cancel the dues of interest payable to may uncle Abbas ibn Abdul Muttalib."

Quran: *"You who believe fear God and write off anything that remains outstanding from lending at interest if you are (true) God and His Messenger. If you repent you may retail your principal do not wrong and you will not be wronged"* (2:278).

TREATMENT OF WIFE (SPOUSE)

Sermon: "Oh people, your wives have a certain right over you and you have a certain right over them. Treat them well and be kind to them for they are your committed partners and committed helpers.

Quran: *"Provide for them the rich according to his income and the poor according to his means, a provision according to the custom. This is an obligation for those who act kindly"* (2:236). *"Treat them politely even if you dislike them,. Perhaps you dislike something in which God has placed much good"* (4:19).

WARNING ABOUT SATAN

Sermon: "Beware of Satan, he is desperate to divert you from the worship of God so beware of him in matters of your way of life."

Quran: *"Verily Satan is an enemy to you so treat him as an enemy. He only invites his followers that they may become companions of the blazing fire"* (35:6).

BROTHERHOOD

Sermon: "Oh you people listen carefully. All the believers are brothers. You are not allowed to the things belonging to another Muslim unless he give it to you willingly."

Quran: *"Believers are but brothers so set things right between your brothers and fear God so that you may find mercy"* (49:10).

SUPERIORITY IS ONLY IN PIETY AND SUBMISSION

Sermon: "Oh people, no one is higher than the other unless he is higher in obedience to God. No Arab is superior to a non-Arab except in piety."

Quran:*"The most honored among you in the sight of God is (he who is) the most righteous of you and God has full knowledge and is will acquainted (with all things)"* (49:134). *"Who can be better in religion than he who submits his whose self to God, does good and follows the ways of Abraham for God did take Abraham for a friend"* (4:125).

IN ORDER TO BE SUCCESSFUL WE MUST OBEY BOTH GOD AND HIS MESSENGER

Sermon: "Oh people, reflect on my words. I leave behind me two things, the Quran and my example and if you follow these, you will not fail."

Quran: *"And obey God and the Messenger so that you may receive mercy"* (3:132).

OBSERVE THE PILLARS OF ISLAM

Sermon: "Listen to me carefully. Worship God and offer prescribed prayer, observe fasting in the month of Ramadan and pay the poor-due."

Quran:*"And establish the prescribed prayer, practice regular charity and bow down with those who bow down"* (2:43). *"Oh you who believe, fasting is prescribed to you as it was prescribed to those before you that you may learn self-restraint"* (2:183).

DUTIES REGARDING THOSE WORKING UNDER US

Sermon: "Oh people, be mindful of those who work under you. Feed and clothe them as you feed and clothe yourselves."

Quran: *"Act kindly just as God treated you kindly"* (28:77). *"God has *favored some of you over their provisions to those whom their right hand controls so that they become equal (partners) in it. Would they thus disclaim God's favor"* (16:71).

MUHAMMAD WAS THE LAST PROPHET

Sermon: "Oh people, no prophet or messenger will come after me and no new faith will emerge."

Quran: "Muhammad is not the father of any of you men but he is God's Messenger and the Seal of Prophets. God is aware of everything" (33:40).

OUR DUTY IS TO SPREAD THE MESSAGE OF THE PROPHET (QURAN)

Sermon: "All those who listen to me shall pass on my words to others and those to others again (and people did).

Quran: "Oh Messenger, communicate whatever has been sent down to you by your Lord. If you do not do so, you will not have conveyed his message" (5:67).

Sermon: Have I conveyed the Message of God to you? asked the Prophet facing towards the heavens. The audience answered in one voice, "You have, God is the witness."

Quran: As the Messenger finished the following revelation came to him, *"Today I have perfected your religion for you, completed my favors upon you and have chosen for you Islam as the way of life for you"* (5:3).

7 RE-DEFINING ISLAMIC CONCEPTS: AN AGENDA FOR MUSLIMS OF NORTH AMERICA

Islam does not need redefinition. But for sure, the application of its concepts in a changing world need to be re-explained in the language of time for better understanding. The problem is as someone put it— how to recover Islam from the debris of its past. By past, it is meant 1,300 years and by the debris, it is meant all the personal, cultural, tribal, and other influences which have covered and mixed with the beautiful and pure religion of al-Islam, the way of life, of peace within and without (with surroundings) by submitting and surrendering our will to the Will of our Creator. Do all Muslims know the will of God and if told, accept it?

The religion has become like the story of four blind men which I read in my childhood who set out to find what the elephant was like. They all returned after touching one organ of the elephant to share their information. The one who touched the leg of the elephant said it was like a big tree. "No," said the other one who touched the side, "it is like a flat wall." The one who touched the tail defined the elephant as a rope. The fourth one who dared to climb up and touch the big ear, compared it to a big leaf of a tree. Then they all started fighting over their version. Non-Muslim becomes Muslim by the grace of God. What kind of Muslim should he become? Sunni or Shia and take one of the twenty sub groups of the former or twelve sub groups of the later? Should he wear the dress of the country he was born in (meeting all the requirements) or adopt the Islamic dress of another Muslim country? If it is not necessary for a new Muslim to go into such details, and just remain a Muslim, why cannot this also be applied to the existing Muslims.

Among the present day Muslims, two types worry me and are equally dangerous examples in showing Islam .

Supermarket Muslims: The majority of Muslims are becoming like this. They have a Muslim name and are usually born to a Muslim family, middle class but aspiring to join the western upper class. They don't pray on a daily basis, but usually on Fridays and always on the Festival days to the prescribed prayer. They do not fast for the fear of becoming weak (or have another excuse). They usually do not calculate the poor-due, but do give charity to ward off evil. They sometimes go for *umrah* but hardly go for the *hajj*. They are careful not to eat pork or take alcoholic beverages, but don't worry about the modest dress and the free intermixing of the sexes. They fail to identify themselves when among non-Muslims and fail to sympathize with the sufferings of the Muslim community (ummah). They are apologetic to non-Muslims about the behavior of fellow Muslims. They themselves do not come to a Sunday school or Islamic Study Circle but want their children to have a religious scholar train them or attend a Sunday school. In my opinion, these are not reformed Muslims, but deformed or confused Muslims; confused about their knowledge of Islam and correct application of it. They have weak faith. To me they deserve the most attention from practicing Muslims.

THE RITUALISTIC KNOWLEDGEABLE MUSLIM BUT DEVOID OF A MORAL CODE.

Here we see a group of Muslims who do practice acts of worship and I pray may Allah accept them and reward them. Their problem is that they have not come out of the first one hundred years of Islam. To that knowledge (without its essence), they have added all the cultural, personal, and regional biases and practices of the following 1,300 years and call it the Islamic Way of Life. So their main obsession is whether to eat with their hand (as the Messenger did) or with a fork, how long their beard should be or the clothing worn, for which ailment honey should be used, and so on. Many of them, while still practicing rituals, do not consider lying, backbiting, gossiping, ill temper, etc. as an un-Islamic Way of Life. They are careful about the permissible and prohibited foods,, but in doing so, are not careful about injuring the feelings of other Muslims. Many such Muslims are so proud of their knowledge and piety that they do not even consider other non-practicing Muslims worthy of their attention and friendship, but they are always available to give missionary work to non-Muslims.

In between the two major groups is the third group which is trying to understand Islam and translate it into a simple common language for the understanding of both groups and non-Muslims. To this group, the philosophy of Islam and its modern application is as important as the rituals of Islam. Unfortunately, the third group is not well-accepted by the first two groups. Now, do we need a new organization? Not really.

The existing organizations should clearly define their aims and modus operandi. They are a mixture of ultra conservatives and ultra liberals. They also change their stand according to need. They fail to address the problems of the Muslim community. Therefore, the majority of American Muslims do not see these organizations truly representing them, thus they do not join them. The elders of such organizations in America are usually immigrant Muslims and their children born in this country. They see things differently. Similarly, 60 percent of the immigrant Muslims do not take into account the 40 percent of native Muslims. Thus, they live in two different worlds. Many of such organizations are more preoccupied with being accepted as moderate and harmless Muslims by the media and non-Muslims than standing up for an Islamic cause with Truth, therefore disassociating themselves with the voice or voices of the rest of the Islamic world.

THE INGREDIENTS OF A STRONG MUSLIM ORGANIZATION REPRESENTING AMERICAN MUSLIMS

They must, first of all, have a "think tank" consisting of about fifty scholars representing all sects, all regions, all ethnic backgrounds, businesses, professions, men, women, youth, from Muslims in prison to the highest official. There should be an Amir (Imam or whatever) with the line of succession and an executive body and a council of Muslim elders to work toward reviving the caliphate.

Sources of financing and ongoing income must be clearly defined. To begin with, such an organization may need $500,000 but to run it would require a minimum of one million dollars a year.

There should be a central office (National Headquarters) with regional offices in each state.

There should be no reduplication of work or rediscovering the wheel. Many organizations for the last twenty-five years have laid some groundwork and their experience is available. This data should be fully utilized. In fact, if some of them want to merge with this new organization, they should be welcomed but not at the expense of changing the agenda.

The main agenda is to prepare Muslims to be knowledgeable about Islam, to be strong, to be able to show it by example and practice, to be able to defend and propagate Islam and to be able to raise Muslims among the children after the present day concerned leaders leave the scene in the next twenty to thirty years. The specific roles are: 1) education of children at schools, mosque, and home, 2) evaluation of practices of Islam by their adults in rituals and morals, 3) financial, social, medical needs of the community to make them strong, healthy and socially happy, 4) representing Islam in the media, government policies and in the text books, 5) missionary work to non-Muslims sharing the gift, 6) bring closer cooperation with Muslims outside the U.S.A. to be able to understand their issues, and to be able to keep them, irrespective whether we love or hate their rules, and 7) be part of the American mainstream, to be able to vote in elections and speak on their issues of concern, as a united Muslim voice.

8 SOME COMMON MISCONCEPTIONS ABOUT SHI'ISM

T he centuries-old Shia-Sunni differences are the major obstacle to Muslim unity. These differences have always been fanned by the enemies of Islam to their benefit. Unfortunately, some so-called Muslim scholars on their payroll have also played a key role in keeping these differences alive.

Although I was born into a Sayyid Sunni family, I did not know of many differences while growing up as a child. Our families always respected Imam Hussayn (peace be upon him) and his parents and participated in ceremonies marking the anniversary of his martyrdom (the 10th day of the month of Muharram which is called Ashura) by reciting the first chapter of the Quran (al-Fatihah) and other chapters and verses of the Quran and fasted on the ninth and tenth days of that month.

Now when I give lectures on Islam to non-Muslims, one of the questions they always ask me is if I am Shia or Sunni. I ask them if they know the difference. They have no knowledge, other than what has been given to them by the media. So they say Shias are the ones who are the bad guys, the militant version of Islam, and cause all the trouble in the Middle East these days.

These non-Muslim American audiences of mine are surprised to learn that some of the known tyrants like Saddam Hussain and troublemakers like the PLO and Hamas are all Sunnis, just as they are surprised to learn that Tariq Aziz (Iraq's Foreign Minister) is Christian and not a Muslim.

This is what I say to them about Shi'ites.

"If Ali Ibn Talib (cousin of Prophet Muhammad) was a Shia, then I am a Shia. If he was a Sunni, then I am a Sunni (i.e., a follower of Prophet Muhammad (ص)).

In Islam there are five recognized schools of Divine Law: 1) Hanafi; 2) Shafi; 3) Maliki; 4) Hanbali and 5) Jafari. The first four are called Sunni, and the fifth one, who in addition to following sayings and actions of Prophet Muhammad (ص), also follows those of Ali and consider him as the rightful successor of the Prophet, are called Shia . The first four have many major theological differences among themselves and according to a Christian friend of mine, "The only time Sunnis are united is when they are fighting Shias."Shi'ism started as a political movement (Shia means follower or partisan) to help Ali become successor of Muhammad (ص).

Around every successful popular figure, there are some admirers whose own future interests rest with the rise of their leader. Thus in Indiana, we have "Friends of Lugar Club", who are hoping that some day Senator Richard Lugar will become a US President. Nationally, we now have a "Hillary Rodham Clinton Fan Club" with 4, 000 members! Thus, there were the Followers of Ali Club which later on became a political movement. During the initial battles with unbelievers, Ali, the Sword of Islam, was in the forefront and defeated and killed many of their leaders whose children and grandchildren, even when they became Muslims, always remembered who killed their father (animosity).

Ali was raised by Prophet Muhammad as a child so he knew Islam very well. Thus, when he became a judge, his judgments were based on strict Islamic principles, much to the disappointment of many who expected him to be lenient to the rich and powerful. He was so well respected and trusted by both Caliph Abu Bakr and Umar, that in difficult cases they asked his opinion.

Nevertheless, I tell my non-Muslim audience that both Shia and Sunni have many things in common. They both believe in One God (Allah), follow the same Prophet Muhammad (ص) as the last Prophet, offer five daily prescribed prayers, perform the prescribed fast in the month of Ramadan, go to Mecca for the pilgrimage (*hajj*), read the same Quran, and pay the poor-due.

However, my answers can only satisfy my uninformed non-Muslim audience. The Sunni brothers, misguided by western propaganda, who are ready to embrace non-Muslims (especially the white ones), in the pretext of invitation to Islam, will not do so for Shia. They are ignorant Sunnis. Our job as a missionary should be to invite both groups to the true Islam and not chase them out. There is a movement in the Sunni world to have Shias labeled as disbelievers. I have been told that Shaykh Bin Baz of Saudi Arabia has declared an edict that the meat of the People of Book (Jews and Christians) is permissible for Sunni Muslims to eat but not the meat slaughtered by Shias.

There are scholars on both sides, like Imam Khomeini and Shaykh Shaltut of al-Azhar who have done their best to minimize these differences and bring unity, but it is not working due to the misinformation prevailing in the common masses of Sunnis about Shi'ism. Thus I am listing their misconceptions of Shia belief and practices. For answers, I have consulted two Shia scholars in America., Dr. A. S. Hashim of Washington and Imam Muhammad Ali Elahi of Detroit.

Professor Seyyed Hossein Nasr wrote to me "to ignore and not waste time in responding to such wrong allegations." He also mentioned that "a great deal of money and effort is being spent in the last few years to fan the fire of hatred between Shia and Sunni in the Persian Gulf region with obvious political and economical fruits for powers to-be." However, in the interest of Islamic unity, I must deal with the questions rather than shun them. Please note that Imam Jafar (peace be upon him), founder of the Shia school of law, was the teacher of Imam Abu-Hanifa (peace be upon him).

Misconception #1: Shias have a different Quran. They add another 10 chapters to the original Quran.

Response: Not true. I have checked many times Quran kept in Shia homes and mosques. I still find it the same as the original Quran. More recently, I took care of an Iranian lady patient hospitalized here. I saw a copy of the Quran by her side. I borrowed it from her and browsed through cover to cover. In Arabic it was the same as our Quran. Of course, since I did not know the Persian language, I can't say much about the translation. It is a sin to even say that the Quran can be changed or added to by Shia when it is protected by God.

Misconception #2: Some Shia consider Ali as God.

Response: Not true. It is disbelief to even think of such a thing. During the time of Ali, some pagan groups called Gholat did consider Ali as Lord. When he found out, they were burned to death. Alawis of Syria may have a similar belief, but they are non-Muslims, neither Shia nor Sunni.

Misconception #3: Shias have different declarations of faith and they add to the call to prescribed prayer.

Response: The declaration to become a Muslim, as administered to non-Muslims, is the same. Some Shia add to themselves, "Ali is a friend of God (ص) or Ali is a spiritual leader of God," after the call to prescribed prayer, but not as part of the call to prescribed prayer.

Misconception #4: Shias do not perform *sunnah* prayers. *Sunnah* prayers are non obligatory prayers performed by Prophet Muhammad.

Response: Shia do ,perform non-obligatory prayers, 36 cycles per day in total, but call it *nawafil* and not *sunnah*.

Misconception #5: Some Shia believe the Angel Gabriel made a mistake and prophethood was meant for Ali and not Muhammad (ص).

Response: Not true. No Shia thinks of such false claims. "Only demented minds think of such questions."

Misconception #6: Shias slander and ridicule the first three caliphs (Abu Bakr, Umar and Uthman) and Prophet Muhammad's wife, Ayisha.

Response: Shia consider the first three caliphs as great companions and good Muslim administrators, but not spiritual leaders (imams). Imam Jafar Sadiq, whose mother and grandmother came from the line of Abu Bakr, said of Abu Bakr, "He gave me birth twice." Ayisha is respected by Shias as the "Mother of Believers," as Ali respected her when he sent her back from Basra to Madinah after the Battle of the Camel. If some Shia do slander the three caliphs and Ayisha, they do it out of ignorance and should ask God's forgiveness.

Misconception # 7: Shias combine all five prayers into one prayer in the evening.

Response: Not true. In Shia mosques, whether in Iran or the USA, all five daily prayers are performed. Some working Shia do combine noon and afternoon and evening and night, but Shia scholars recommend performing them separately. Such combinations may not be ideal, but better than not praying at all. How can a Sunni who does not pray at all be better than a Shia who combines prayers?

Misconception # 8: Shias do not pay *zakat* (poor-due).

Response: Not true. They not only pay 2.5% left over from savings as *zakat*, but also an additional 20% as *khums* or general charity.

However, they prefer to pay directly to the needy rather than to a corrupt Sunni government.

Misconception #9: Shias practice temporary marriages (*mutah*).

Response: *Mutah* (temporary marriages) was allowed during the time of Prophet Muhammad (ص) and he himself practiced it. Ibn Zubayr was born out of the temporary marriage. Later on Caliph Umar prohibited it due to social reasons as the Islamic world was rapidly expanding. Shias discourage mutah but do not consider it prohibited. Some do abuse this. As a temporary privilege during travel, it is better than adultery.

Misconception #10: They consider Imams infallible and above the prophets.

Response: Not true. All prophets are born Prophet but as mentioned in Quran about Abraham that after passing the test, a prophet becomes a leader (Imam). Imams are carriers of the message of Islam. Shias consider Ali only as an Imam, but Muhammad (ص) is the Prophet (*nabi*), Messenger (*rasul*) and leader (*imam*).

With the little knowledge I have, I have tried to do my best as a Sunni in defending my Shia brothers in Islam with the hope and prayer to God Almighty that He will "*instill love in the heart of the believers*" and bring us closer to each other so that we jointly can fight our common enemy, Satan and his followers.

May God forgive my mistakes in this article and this book (*amin*).

9 THE FUTURE OF ISLAM IN AMERICA

The basic question is, "What is the future of Islam in North America?" While living in the present, we do not see the future, but we are concerned about the future as whatever we do now will affect our future. We are not the first wave of Muslims who have come to this country. There have been at least two or three different waves of Muslims who have come before us and they were not able to establish Islam for whatever reason.

The first wave of Muslims came or were brought in as slaves from Africa two hundred years ago. They could not establish themselves as Muslims as they were oppressed. They were brought in chains and left on plantations in total slavery. Their religion was changed. Their names were changed. Their social structure was broken. They were not allowed to practice their religion. We do not blame them for not being able to establish Islam.

The second wave came after WW I from the Balkan States and Lebanon to what used to be the Ottoman Empire. These Muslims were settled in the midwest and northeast, including areas like Dearborn, Toledo, Chicago and Detroit. They were again more concerned at that time in establishing themselves economically and socially. Religion was not on their minds at that time. They melted away in the melting pot.

It is heartening to note that many of the descendants of the first two waves are now coming back to the fold of Islam and helping establish Islam in cooperation with the third wave which includes the immigrant Muslims coming to this country since the 1950s and constitution sixty percent (60%) of the six million, present-day American Muslims. Many of the Afro-Americans are now finding their roots in Islam, reverting to Islam, and asserting themselves as Muslims.

We also must learn some lessons from the past, of a glorious Muslim empire in Andalusia (Spain). For seven hundred years, Muslims ruled that country, but the were wiped out after the Inquisition. If we analyze what happened in this situations, including other areas of the world where Muslims are in the minority, after being there for many years, we will understand that there were several reasons for them not to be able to establish Islam in the land forever, as we will see in the Muslim countries like Turkey or Egypt. The main reason was the lack of unity among Muslims .

In Spain, they created a class structure of Muslims of Arab descent, the Berbers and the native Spaniards, and these classes did not live on an equal basis. This was against Islam. Second, they were not able to practice Islam collectively, but more individually. Islam is a religion that has to be practiced collectively, and only then is the social fabric established: a thread by itself is not a nation. Third, Islamic education on an individual level was not there, but there was more emphasis on secular and technical education. Fourth, too much emphasis was given to culture, whether in the form of art, music, dress or food, but not enough on defense. Although culture is necessary for the survival of the soul, defense is necessary for the survival of the body. One cannot live without the other. Finally, the most important reason that these civilizations were destroyed was that they failed to invite others to Islam. Invitation to Islam is not a luxury, but a necessity and a tool for survival.

While discussing the future of Islam in North America, we must examine the parameters of a good future. If we judge the future by numbers, yes, it is true that the number of Muslims has tremendously increased in this country. When I came here nearly a quarter of a century ago, there were not more than fifty thousand (50,000) Muslims, and now there are over six million. Nevertheless, if we look at the world map, the number of Muslims is over a billion; however, they hardly have any strength in that number.

It is the quality of Muslims that is important, rather than the number itself. The quality of Muslims who were in the minority and out numbered in the Battle of Badr by three to one, but they were able to succeed with the conviction *"that they are the best nation created for mankind."*

If you look at the number by the number of mosques and minarets, yes, it is true that have also increased. In 1969 there were not more than fifty (50) mosques in the country, and now there are fourteen hundred (1,400). However, unless we have a social structure to protect the mosques, these buildings by themselves cannot defend themselves.

In 1914, when the Russian Army moved into the Muslim part of the USSR from Tajikistan to Tashkent, there were twenty-four thousand mosques (24,000) in those lands. The Red Army destroyed most of them. In seventy (70) years of Communist rule, there were only four hundred (400) left and most of them were lost except for prescribed prayers.

We see among the Christian churches that when the community moves out or has financial problems, they have to sell their churches and move to a different location. Hopefully, we will not come to a state that our Muslim community around a mosque will disappear, leaving only the beautiful minaret which will be purchased by another religion to be converted to their temple.

Although our number is very similar to those of Jewish people in this country, we have no comparison in strength in terms of economic, political and educational strength. We do not have any Congressmen or Senators. We do not control university boards or faculties. We do not have a single factory or financial institution which is able to employ Muslims in large numbers. Therefore, we cannot judge the future of Islam by looking at the number of Muslims praying on earth or attending the conventions and bazaars of ISNA. There have to be deeper indicators of our strength.

Many of the Muslims, especially of immigrant origin, are embroiled in preserving the ethnic culture, but this ethnic culture, whether in the form of social parties, music shows, dress shows, is nothing but a passing show. After this generation of Muslims has passed away, our children and youth of immigrant parents will not be able to sustain that ethnic culture. There will be only two cultures left for Muslims: an Islamic culture and the American culture.

What about our health and physical strength? Muslims, in my opinion, are not keeping themselves in physical shape, either. Most of our parties involve nothing but sitting down, making chit-chat, eating very rich foods and then going to bed. The incidence of coronary artery disease, diabetes and many chronic conditions is increasing. We are not doing exercise nor are we watching our nutrition.

I am saying all this that if our neighbors decide to do the ethnic cleansing, as it is happening in Bosnia, twenty years from now, will we be prepared to defend our women and children? Or, if the United Nations and Bosnian government request the Muslims of North America to come and help them, are we in physical shape to go there and help them in their war? A healthy Muslim is the backbone of a healthy community.

It is true that our family and our youth are our future. Muslim elders, scholars, writers and leaders of the present generation are now in their fifties. In the next twenty to twenty-five years, this generation, which is bearing the task of trying to establish Islam, will pass away. Unless we have created a new grassroots leadership which will replace us, there will be a vacuum.

Therefore, to establish our future, we must establish the Muslim youth. Our fear is that it is possible that many of our Muslim youth will be lost to the community by one way or another. I hope that this does not happen. The reasons for my fear are as such:

The USA is a melting pot. The heat is enough of the social peer pressure that people do get melted down in their values. They get lost. They may not be able to preserve their Islamic identity and outlook the way it should be in a pure form. It is possible that a new revised, modern and reformed version of Islam and Muslims will emerge which will be based more on secular lines with "modern" thinking than basic Islamic teachings. We see this in many civilizations who have pursued the line of modernization without deep thinking, whether it is in Turkey or Iran during the days of the Shah.

The second fear is that of their being lost with intermarriages. Unless we encourage Muslim youth to marry only Muslims when they reach that age and make that decision, it is possible that the future generation may be lost. Although it is permitted for a Muslim man to marry a woman of the People of the Book, there are several problems related to this.

Unless his wife becomes a practicing Muslim, the future of the children and their children to remain Muslim is not guaranteed. If there is a divorce in the family, which does happen frequently, then the custody of the child goes to the mother, who will remains a Jew or a Christian.

More important, the question is what will happen to Muslim girls if all the Muslim boys choose to marry People of the Book? Muslim women ate not allowed to marry non-Muslim men, and if they do, they would not be able to maintain Islam in their children, whose fathers are non-Muslims. Therefore, development and maintenance of intact Muslim families is the key to the survival of Islam in the USA.

My third concern about youth is regarding their education. I am not talking only of secular education, rather Islamic education. Parents have this attitude to drop their kids off at Sunday school and for it to provide a full Islamic education. In two hours a week, one cannot counteract the forty hours of secular education and secular ideas. Therefore, Sunday schools with a lack of funds and resources are not able to do the right job, either.

The result is that most of the education which the Muslim youth receive is superficial and "hearsay" rather than basic didactic Islamic education, unless some of them study on their own. With the lack of true education, our outlook about issues may change, and we may develop an attitude that "there is nothing wrong in this" as there is no mention in the Quran of such issues. This acceptance of certain practices and values of the society, unless it is confirmed by the Quran and *sunnah*, will become part of Islam, or at least of the practicing habit of the people. This is how cultural Islam develops .

Thus, we must emphasize in-depth, basic education for all Muslim youth, irrespective of their family background, whether their parents have been practicing or not practicing, or which school of thought they belong to, or what their socioeconomic structure is, in order to develop a nation of Muslims who have knowledge of Islam and are practicing Islam in order to preserve it.

With regard to secular education, the parents have a role to play in directing their youth's educational future. The desire of most parents that children become doctors or engineers is not always necessary. There are other fields that Muslims should go into, including journalism, law, politics, accounting, banking, agriculture and teaching. In order for us to have a significant impart on the decision-making process in this country, we need to have a lobby in each organization with grassroots support. .

We must keep youth together, whether in the form of Islamic Boy Scouts, Islamic Girl Scouts, or Muslim Youth of North America . When we create such organizations, we should not just give them an umbrella to do their own thing in their own way without parental supervision. If Muslim youth organizations will do similar things as non-Muslim organizations will do, under the umbrella disguise of Islam, there will be no difference in them and non-Muslim organizations. There has to be adult supervision. The rules of the Shariah should still apply to them, and they must follow their daily routines of Islam.

Parents should support these organizations with their involvement and with their money. More important, Muslims, youth and adult men and women should have a sense of self-esteem which tells them that no matter how they are humiliated, defamed and ridiculed by the media, they are on the right path, a path which has been chosen for them, and neither do they eat pork, nor drink alcohol, nor listen to sexually suggestive rock music, nor be involved in an intimate mixing of sexes, because of their conviction of "b*eing the best of mankind that have been raised to enjoin what is good and forbid what is wrong—and they believe in God."*

There is a fear that an American version of Islam may emerge among American Muslims, especially the youth. Our hope is that this will not happen, and Muslims in America will raise themselves from nationalism of all kinds and pride themselves on being just Muslims, caring for and loving all other Muslims around the world.

Our love for our family should not reflect in providing for them all the worldly amenities like clothing, food, house, car, TV/VCR, etc., but more importantly safeguarding their future in both worlds. "*O you who believe, save yourself and your family from a fire.*" In this regard, Islam and the education of Muslim women is a matter of prime importance! The first school for a Muslim child is going to be his or her home. What kind of "teacher" has he?

Yes, our hope is in our family, and hope is in our youth. We hope that our families will remain intact as Muslim families and will be able to preserve Islam in their homes and propagate it outside the home. We hope the youth of today are better Muslims than their parents were when they were young. It is this hope that gives me the satisfaction that the adults of tomorrow will also be better adults than they are today, in terms of practicing Islam and love and unity among themselves.

We also hope that they will be better prepared to deal with situations and American issues. The present-day Muslim adults are living in isolation, not being part of the mainstream American society. We hope that the Muslim youths who are born and raised in this society will be able to mix with non-Muslims with conviction, maintaining their own identity in order to offer solutions for the country in which they are born.

Society as such is on a decline because of its moral decay and breakup of the social fabric. We hope that Islam in its pure form, when practiced by a large number of Americans, will be able to save America from such decay by offering a viable social alternative. The future of Islam is not at stake, but that of those who profess to be its followers is.

> *By the token of time*
> *the mankind is at loss*
> *except as those who have*
> *true belief and pure actions*
> *and join together in the*
> *mutual teaching of truth*
> *and patience.*

EPILOGUE
THE STORY OF MY BEARD

My beard is not that important. What I do with that cover is more important and what's in my heart is the most important.

My first ten years of post puberty life were spent in a Muslim country. I used to shave daily as it was assumed there that only religious fanatics or uneducated backward folks had a beard, and I was neither.

Twenty years ago when I came to the United States I was surprised to observe that many non-Muslims here i.e. musicians, hippies, even intellectual professors and shrinks, had beards. So out of fashion, I started experimenting on my face with different shapes and length of beard.

In 1979, with the Iranian revolution, growing a beard became a way of identification for many young Muslims. It was a common scene for eight years, to see on TV bearded folks marching in the streets of Tehran. In fact in those days a Sikh was mistaken as a Muslim and shot dead in Boston. Well! I had anticipated the revolution in advance, so when it came I already had a nice full beard.

But certain strange things started to happen to me. My friends, out of respect, started to elevate me out of proportion, expecting no mistakes from me or else considered me a fanatic revolutionary and scarcely detested me.

When I looked at my bearded Muslim colleagues, for some it was the final compliment to their beautiful Islamic personality, and for others, the beard was all they had. When I asked my mentor, a friend of fifteen years, a known Islamic scholar above seventy years of age, as to why he did not grow a beard knowing that it was a tradition of Prophet Muhammad (ص)? He said, " When I used to have a beard, I just became a holy person to a few devout people. They started kissing my beard and my hand, while turning a deaf ear to what I was saying or writing. My views were liberal and did not match with my beard so some thought I must be a hypocrite."

The happiest incident connected with my beard happened when I was in a New York hotel. I ordered a plain omelet for breakfast. The American waitress, looked at me and said " You look like a Muslim, and I know this omelet is not plain. It has ham in it, so would you like to order something else?" I thanked her for saving me from eating pork and I thanked God for making me look like a Muslim.

Then a stage came when I could not figure out who among my friends were sincere towards me. Those who pretended that they loved me were sometime backbiting against me. So I decided to try an experiment. At the peak of my "holiness" —by that time I was a writer, author, speaker on Islam—I decided to shave my beard to the shock of many, including my family members.

There were many who were obviously pleased, i.e. my three year old and nine year old, to them it did not hurt when I kissed them. However those who were scared of my beard really liked me clean shaved. My chief of medicine asked," Is this a message ?" I replied in his own tone, "No I am still a terrorist, in fact more dangerous now. I used to be Khomeini, now I am Saddam Hussain." One old patient had an interesting comment. He said, "Doc! You look naked without your beard" and I did "feel naked." Those Muslims who objected to me shaving my beard were the ones who did not like me with or without the beard, so it did not matter much. Someone commented, it added 10-15 years to my life (i.e. looked younger), but did I?

I observed my friends and Muslims who loved me truly, continued to love me without my beard, though in their heart they wished I had never shaved. One such message I received from a friend, Imam Siraj Wahhaj when I met him at a convention. Although shocked, he smiled and embraced me, without saying a word, touched my face, where my beard used to be, telling me without words that he loved me and my beard both.

My decision to grow back my beard was none of the above observation, nor demands of my patients that I should look more dignified, but a question I asked myself. How do I want to look when I am being laid to rest in the coffin. I looked at my former picture and the mirror and the answer was obvious. I am fully clothed now!!

BIBLIOGRAPHY

Amnesty Action. Iraq's war on its children. March, 1989.

Amnesty Action. November/December, 1988; September/October, 1988; January/February, 1989.

Amnesty International Annual Report, 1988.

Athar, Shahid.

"Agonies of a Muslim Living in a Non-Muslim Society." *Minaret*, New York, March, 1983.

"Alcohol, Drugs and Muslim Youth Lecture." United States Cultural Center, Karachi, Pakistan, 1990. Published in *Noorul Islam* and Crescent International.

"Blueprint for Efficiency and Excellence for Muslims." Friday Sermon, Islamic Center, Plainfield, Indiana, May, 1987.

"Communication within the Family and the Community." ISGI Seminar, Plainfield, Indiana, 1993.

"Contribution of Muslim Scientists and Physicians of the Past." MCC, Chicago, February 11, 1990 and Purdue University, 1991.

"Death and Dying in Islam." Lecture at St. Vincent Hospital Hospice to Indiana Chaplins, March, 1994.

"Effect of Prohibited Food, Intoxicants and Ingredients on Human Hormone and Behavior." *Islamic Perspective*, October, 1988.

"Fallout from the Cairo Population Conference, The." Friday Sermon at al-Fajr Mosque, Indianapolis, Indiana and the Islamic Center, Plainfield, Indiana.

"Future of Islam in America." Published as "Our Family, Our Youth, Our Hope for the Future." *Pakistan Link,* September, 1994.

"Health Concerns of Muslims in North America." Lecture at MCC, Chicago, September, 1986.

"Health from Quran and Sunnah." *Islamic Horizon*, April, 1984.

"How to Survive as a Muslim in a Non-Muslim Society." Lecture at the Islamic Society of New Jersey, May, 1993.

"Influencing the Behavior of Children and Their Parents." Presented at APPNA, MYNA and AMSS Seminars.

"Influencing the Behavior of Muslim Youth and Their Parents." Seminar on Organizational Behavior, AMSS at IIIT, Washington, D. C. Also published in *Crescent International*, Toronto and The Message International, New York.

"Invitation to Islam." Friday Sermon at al-Fajr Mosque, Indianapolis, Indiana, 1992.

"Islam in North America." Lecture at World Muslim Congress, Karachi, Pakistan, June 22, 1989.

"Islamic Perspective in Stress Management." *Hamdard Medicus*, 1989.

"Islamic Perspectives in Medical Ethics." *Hamdard Medicus*, June, 1989.

"Islamic Solutions to the Secularization of Higher Education." Presented at ACURA Conference at Ball State University, November, 1993.

"Judaism, Christianity, and Islam: Can They Peacefully Coexist?" Delivered at the Rotary International, Peru, Indiana as part of the Great Decisions" lectures, March 1, 1990.

"Love and Unity for the Cause of God." Lecture delivered at the Islamic Society of West Virginia, February 19, 1989. Published in *Pakistan Link*, 1993.

"Lying and Falsehood: A Disease of the Heart." Friday Sermon in PTS.

"Lying: A Disease" Friday Sermon delivered at the Islamic Center, Plainfield, Indiana, 1989.

"Malcolm X: The Prince of Islam in North America." Friday Sermon. Published in the *Bulletin of Affiliation*, Washington, DC, October, 1993.

"Marital Relationships and Mutual Rights in Islam." Friday Sermon, al-Fajr mosque, 1993.

"Misconceptions About Islam." Lecture at churches and radio inter view. Published as *25 Most Frequently Asked Questions About Islam*.

"Mixing Religion and Politics." Presented at the Jewish Community Relations Council Seminar, Indianapolis, November, 1993.

"Mixing Religion and Politics." Published in *The Message*, August, 1994.

"Obstacles in the Way of Cohesion of Muslim Community in North America." *Crescent International*, March , 1988 and Noorul Islam, 1992.

"Obstacles to the Cohesion of Muslim Unity." Presidential address on the state of Muslim Communities. Annual function of Islamic Society of Greater Indianapolis, April 22, 1987.

"Peace Through Submission." Key Note Address at the Muslim Society, University of Texas at Commence, January, 1986.

"Practicing God Consciousness." Friday Sermon. Published in *Bulletin of Affiliation* in PTS.

"Practicing Piety." Adopted from the Friday Sermon delivered at the Islamic Center, Plainfield, Indiana.

"Redefining Islamic Concepts." Presented at a conference, "Redefining Islamic Concepts in the Year 2000 CE, Los Angeles, 1991.

"Reflections on Bosnia and the Holocaust." Speech, Indianapolis, Indiana Peace and Justice Center, April 19, 1993.

"Reflections on the Eurocentric View of History." Prescribed at the Second Parliament of the World's Religions, Chicago, Illinois, September 3, 1993. Published in *Crescent International*, Toronto, November 16-30, 1993.

"Reflections on the Gulf War." Lecture at Beth El-Zedeck Hebrew Congregation, Indianapolis, Indiana, January 16, 1991 on the eve of the ground war in the Gulf.

"Religion and Philanthropy." Indiana University Center for Philanthropy, April, 1994.

"Secularization of Higher Education: An Islamic Response." Lecture delivered on November, 1, 1993 at a seminar, "Expression of Religion in American Higher Education." Association of College and University Religious Affairs. Ball State University and Marion College, Indianapolis, Indiana.

"Sex Education: A Guideline for Muslim Youth and Their Parents." *Journal of Islamic Medical Association*, January, 1990.

"Social Concerns for Muslims in North America." New Jersey

Lecture. April 4, 1993.

"Story of My Beard, The." *The Minaret*. Los Angeles, California.

"Taking Islam and Muslims Out of the Closet." Published in *The Message*, February, 1994.

"The Crisis in the Muslim World and the Response of American Muslims." Friday Sermon, Islamic Center, Plainfield, Indiana, February 26, 1993. Lecture at Empowering Muslims Conference. Published in *Muslim World Weekly*, Karachi, October, 1993.

"The Gulf Crisis and American Muslims." Lecture at Beth el-Zedeck Hebrew Congregation, March, 1991.

"The Last Sermon of Prophet Muhammad: Confirmation of the Main Points from the Quran." Friday Sermon delivered at the Islamic Center, Plainfield, Indiana, 1990.

"The Pursuit of Knowledge and Education." Friday sermon at al-Fajr Mosque, Indianapolis, Indiana.

"The Role of Muslim Clergy in Ethical Decision Making in Patient Care." West Virginia University. National Seminar on Medical Ethics, June, 1994.

"Therapeutic Benefits of Ramadan Fasting." *Islamic Horizon*, May, 1984.

"Violation of Human Rights by the Superpowers and Muslim Countries (Friday Sermon). Published in *The Minaret*, Los Angeles, 1992.

"What is Required of Us as Muslims?" Published in **The Bulletin of Affiliation**, Washington, DC, February, 1994.

"Why Muslim? Moral System of Islam vs. Secular Humanism." In *Peace Through Submission*.

Bach, G. R. and R. M. Deutsch. *Pairing: How to Achieve Genuine Intimacy*. New York: Avon Books, 1970.

Caplan, G. Mastery of stress: psychological aspects. *AM J Psychiatry*, 138:413, 1981.

Farrar, Tarikhu. When African kings become chiefs. *Journal of Black Studies*, December, 1992.

Filley, A. C. *Interpersonal Conflict Resolution*. Glenview, IL: Scott, Foresman and Company, 1975.

Flaherty, J. A. and J. A. Richman. Effect of childhood relationships on the adult's capacity to form social supports. *AM J Psychiatry* 143 (7): 851, 1986.

Gelles, R. J. The Family and Its Role in the Abuse of Children. *J Commun Discord* 5:154, 1972.

Gerber, M. Caring for normal and developmentally delayed infants. In I. Jakab (ed.), *Mental Retardation*. New York: Karger Basel, 1982, p. 374.

Ghassan, Salami. *Islam and the West*. Foreign Policy Review.

Haque, S. Nomanul. *Salman Rushdie: Blame Yourself.* New York Times, February 23, 1989.

Holy Quran. Translated by A. Yusuf Ali. Washington DC: Amana Corporation.

Huntington, Samuel. "The Clash of civilizations.". *Foreign Affairs*, Summer, 1993.

Jameelah, Maryam. *Islam and Modernism: Cultural Slavery is Inseparable from Political Slavery*. Lahore, Pakistan: M. Y. Khan.

Khoder, Muhammad. *Islam and Human Rights*. Translated by Zaid al-Hussain. Beirut, Lebanon: Dar Koder.

Kiester, Edwin Jr. and Sally Kiester. How to raise a happy child. *Reader's Digest*, January, 1986.

Lewis, Bernard. *Islam and the West*. Oxford UP, 1993.

May, Earnest. *A Proud Nation*. Textbook of US History.

Mazrui, Ali. A. Satanic verses or a satanic novel? Greenpoint, NY: Council of Muslim Scholars and Leaders of North America.

Miller, Judith. The Challenge of radical islam. *Foreign Affairs*, Spring, 1993.

Nicholi, A. N. Jr. The Adolescent. In Nicholi A. N. Jr. (ed.). *The Harvard Guide to Modern Psychiatry*. Cambridge, MA: Belknap Press of Harvard University Press, 1978, p. 519.

Novak, Michael. The absolute right to free expression and inquiry. *Indianapolis Star*. March 5, 1989.

Pellegrini, R. J. Teaching Effectiveness and Interpersonal Commitment in the Educational Setting: Some Reality Perspectives on Human Development. *Social Studies Review* 22:61, 1983,.

Report of a Medical Mission by Physicians for Human Rights. Winds of death. February, 1989.

Said, Edward. *Culture and Imperialism*. NY: Alfred Knopf, 1993.

Samir, Amin. Eurocentrism. NY: *Monthly Review Press*, 1988.

Shaheen, Jack. *The T. V. Arabs*. Bowling Green State University Press.

Siddique, Dr. Kalim. I*ssues in the Islamic Movement*: 1980-1987.

London: Simon and Schuster.

Szule, Ted. *Hell on Earth*. Amnesty International Publication.

Time Magazine. A cry of desperation. January 9, 1989.

Torgersen, S. Childhood and family characteristics in panic and generalized anxiety disorders. *AM J Psychiatry*, 143 (5):630, 1987.

General Index

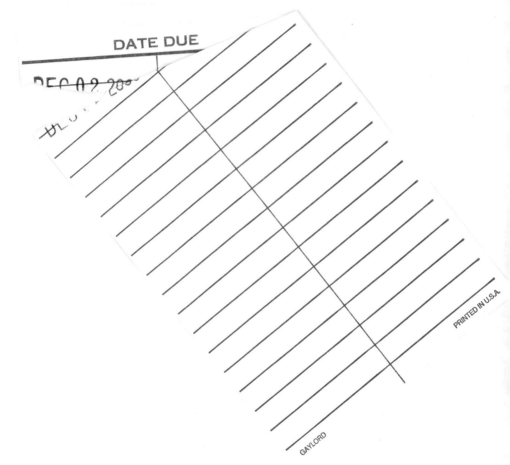